Faith in Hand

Faith in Hand

A Prevailing Light over Darkness

SAMANTHA MARTIN

First edition 2022

Book design by Publishing Push

ISBN 978-1-80227-368-7 (paperback)
ISBN 978-1-80227-369-4 (ebook)

Typeset using Atomik ePublisher from Easypress Technologies

Acknowledgement

Thirty-odd years ago, I went through an unthinkable experience that left me a changed person from who I once was. As the years have gone on since that time, I often pondered the idea of writing all my experiences down one day. I started many years ago but only got as far as writing down the chapter headings. That was until now.

It all began by receiving a heart-wrenching diagnosis that rendered me undergoing surgery along with a clinical watch for five years. Yet another profound experience entered my life. I found myself in a place of contemplation along with what seemed like a barrage of obstacles in my life's path. I seemed to have come to a standstill with no incentive and an uncertainty of what I was going to do next.

That was until I lay awake in my bed one night, thoughts of all nature bombarding my mind: many were negative, which was unlike me, as I tried to look on the positive side as much as I could. As I lay there contemplating my situation, I started regressing back to my childhood, finding myself smiling at the wonderful memories I have of that time. This, of course, is thanks to both of my parents for making those times so memorable. Along with the endless stream of love and devotion I felt from them both every day.

I would like to take this opportunity in expressing immense gratitude and much love to them both for always being by my side and providing solid guidance that I have relied upon on many occasions. Expect the unexpected, they would say, and boy, I did that alright, and so did they.

This phrase will become clearer to you as you read on. Thank you for always standing one step behind me. I'll always love you both forever, the great and the wonderful; that's my mum and dad.

As my thoughts continued that night, I began pondering over what I had thought about doing many years previously, and that was to write a book about all my experiences over the years. The inspirational time was now; it felt right.

The initial fears in opening up about those experiences rose to the surface once again. But with the ongoing support from my husband and both of my girls came the encouragement to speak out. This I want to thank them for with all of my heart. Without their encouragement and support, it's possible this book would still be a figment of my imagination.

My husband has been a massive shining light to me; not only is he my husband, but he is also my best friend and to have him in my life is a total blessing. My love for you is infinite. This, too, can be said for both of my daughters, who have continued to bring immense joy to my life from the time they were born. I am so very proud of the women you have both become. Continue to always shine like the brightest stars, girls, for you have so much to offer everyone and the world around you. I will always love you both forevermore.

Special thanks to my brother and sister for their ongoing words of encouragement.

Also, I would like to extend a huge gesture of gratitude to everyone that helped me in the process of my book. I will be forever thankful.

Finally, I send vibrational love, peace and appreciation to all the souls that have passed over to the spirit world for the guidance they have given me in my daily life over the years.

Introduction

The story you're about to read will take you through passages of the unexplained. A blend of both desirable and unwelcome chapters of my life from a young child to teenage years and beyond. My mind-twisting experiences, placing unchartered events of the unknown in my pathway each night.

Behind the general persona of my young teenage self stood a rather complex individual, juggling day-to-day normality with her connections to the other side. I'm under no illusion that the following will bring trepidation to some and belief from others.

This has been a 30-year-long process for me. I knew the time would come, one day, to speak out about my paranormal experiences, hopefully bringing insight to anyone out there having the same conflict with themselves as I once did.

Fear played a huge part in being one of the reasons why I had not put pen to paper sooner. My biggest reasoning for this was I had two young girls. The thought of them becoming the source of any ridicule left me in no doubt but to leave everything I knew stored away in my memory until a later date. Both of our daughters have now grown into fine, strong, independent women with children of their own, gifting myself and my husband beautiful grandchildren. Their growth has now paved the way for all that I have seen to be told.

My one desire is that this book will bring some clarity and hope for others experiencing the diversity of life that comes in many forms. You need not be alone to face the mysteries of what your eyes may see and your ears may hear. Don't be afraid to bring your own experiences to light; a shared problem is one that is halved.

So, let me take you on a journey that I once had; make of it as you will.

All you will read are my honest accounts of what I have seen, heard and felt, during the years of my life that I will never forget.

Chapter 1

Family

I was born in the early '70s, living in a three-bed terraced house in a popular housing estate with my parents and two elder siblings. My brother was eleven years older, and my sister was ten, so I was the baby of the family. I had always been brought up to believe in God, Jesus and the Holy Ghost. I was a Christian; prayer had been taught to me from an early age. I went to church frequently with both of my parents.

I can always remember as a young child our home being full at all times. Extended family members were visiting daily, whether they were my aunts, uncles, grandma, or nan. It seemed that every day someone visited for a cup of tea and a sandwich around lunchtime, never leaving much before late afternoon. Unfortunately, both of my grandads had passed away. My mum's dad passed before I was born, and my father's dad died when I was two. However, I was lucky enough to have my grandma and nan at hand every day. We were always a strong family unit with countless love and support.

Recollecting some memories from my childhood is hard with being so young, but I will never forget the special relationship that I had with my grandma. To this day, I am unable to explain the connection I had with her. It was just magical.

My relationship with my nan, however, was different in many ways. She was a harsher lady and didn't show emotion so willingly. My grandad Jim was my nan's husband, and he was the softer one out of the two. He used to call me 'copper knob' as my hair had strands of auburn running through it, especially when the sun was out. This leads me nicely to one particular day, which I now know was the start of events that would fill my life with confusion, questioning and not least wonder.

The day started in the usual manner, mainly play for me. The routine of our home became apparent to me at an early age. Dad came home for lunch at the same time every day on weekdays, and we would all have lunch together as normal. On this day, my mum had trouble getting me to stop playing underneath the stairs. They could hear all my chattering; it was as if I was talking to somebody. After some time, mum came out to me and asked who I was talking to.

"Grandad," I said.

As mum recollects it now, she just shrugged it off, thinking it was just the typical imagination of a young child. Little did I know that my grandad Jim had sadly passed away quite some time ago. It wasn't until I became agitated, saying that mum's appearance had made grandad disappear, that mum spoke with dad about what I had previously said to her. They both agreed to sit me down and ask me how I knew this person was grandad. My answer to this was simple. He told me that he was my grandad. They couldn't believe their ears, and from this, the questioning began. Firstly, they asked me what grandad looked like. I described, to the best of my ability, the image of the person I had been talking with. To their utter surprise, I had accurately described my grandad, Jim.

"He called me copper knob."

This blew my parents away. They had never come across a situation like it before, especially not involving their young daughter, and because of this, it was never really spoken about again. The question still often rings in my memory of why grandad came to me that day. Did he have something important to tell me? Was this his way of trying to help me, to ready myself for future events that were to come? I never received the answer for this, but I thank him for the short, treasured moment we had together that day.

As the years went by, my relationship with my grandma grew ever stronger. She looked after me often when my mum went to work. Her speciality was cauliflower cheese, which I had most days for my evening meal. It was delicious. My brother and sister were so much older than me, which meant they used to do their own thing. Often, I was on my own with her. There were a few times that I remember my brother and sister joining us for the evening. My brother had a great relationship with both my grandma and my nan, but my sister's connection was not so good. It never really worked in her favour that I was the baby of the family, and especially having a strong bond with our grandma. This undoubtingly used to annoy the living daylights out of my sister, and particularly when it came down to her boyfriend coming to the house. My sister, being the elder, often took it into her own hands to reprimand me, but this didn't go down well in my grandma's eyes. She often chased my sister around the kitchen table if she had bad-mouthed my grandma in any way.

As well as looking after me in the early evenings whilst my mum was working, we used to go out as a family, taking my grandma with us. One treasured memory was when dad parked the car up alongside a green. All of us were sitting there having a sandwich and a cup of tea around a portable picnic table, engaged in long conversations about all sorts of things. Mum and Dad's tea set was made up of blue plastic cups with a large circular diameter but shallow in depth, with tiny handles to put your finger through.

My grandma, being the lady she was, always held her pinky up in the air whilst holding her cup. She was a very smart-dressed lady, always wearing a diamante broach on the lapel of her jacket. She wore these blue-rimmed glasses that slightly flicked up at the ends. She also had a very distinctive mole placed right in the middle of her cleavage. It resembled a walnut in size and appearance. This mole fascinated me for some reason. Sometimes I'd give it a poke, but the feel of it on my finger made my tummy roll over, so I didn't do that very often.

Unfortunately, I can't remember running around with my grandma. She had bad legs and wore thick stockings to help with support and circulation. My pride of place was sitting on her lap. I have a cherished photograph perfectly capturing us saying cheers, tapping our blue plastic cups together with a smile that would light up any dark day.

Grandma lived in a lovely flat, small but cosy, inside a large building that was warden-assisted with many other residents. The building was situated just up the road from us, which I loved. Alongside this was a play area with a couple of swings, and there were a few shops nearby. These consisted of a hairdresser, a sweet shop and a grocery.

As I grew older, I was able to go and see Grandma on my own. This was the highlight of my day. There was a pretty little pond inside the building on the ground floor with a few goldfish in and a little waterfall echoing the sounds of water within the walls. I would always stand looking at the goldfish first and would often bump into a lady called Mrs Tutt, a petite lady with a soft-spoken voice. She was one of my grandma's friends, so I used to see her often on my visits. She was lovely.

It filled me with joy every time the door opened, and there stood my grandma. We would have a big hug and talk about everything and anything. After this, I would dust her tiny table that used to have a pretty crochet doily placed on the top, along with a beautiful glass multi-coloured fish. I loved that fish. It was difficult for my grandma to bend down to dust these surfaces, so I did it for her. Once I had completed my task for the day, Grandma used to give me some pocket money to go down to the shops to get some sweets. I would skip to my heart's delight all the way down the snake-shaped path; all the while, Grandma would be watching me intently from her window. When it was time for me to go home, we would wave continuously to each other as I went, leaving with a feeling of excitement for tomorrow to come so I could see her again.

After celebrating my grandma's 74th birthday, mum received a telephone call that would devastate our world. My beloved grandma had been taken to hospital with a suspected stroke. Both of my parents went immediately to the hospital and left me in the care of my siblings. On their return, I could see the devastation on my mum's face; Grandma had had a stroke, and rather a bad one at that. The stroke had taken her speech and coordination away, leaving her unable to communicate.

Mum visited every day. Thankfully, Grandma showed some awareness in that she recognized Mum. They held on to one another hands as Mum sat by her bedside. My grandma showed true courage every day, trying her best to communicate but to no avail. In the end, she couldn't even feed herself. This would have devastated my grandma if she had been aware, being the strong, independent, loving woman that she was.

Time went by to the unthinkable moment when my grandma passed away. I can remember my mum telling me that Grandma had gone to heaven, the tears running down her face. I had eight wonderful years with my grandma, and the memories will stay forever etched in my heart. I learnt as I got older that Grandma's passing was not as peaceful as one would have wished. Mum had said that Grandma was scared. She had regained some speech just before her passing, mentioning a dark tunnel that she didn't want to go down. Thankfully this didn't last long.

For the first time in my life, I felt heartbreak and a feeling of loss. I can remember going up to Grandma's building, going inside and just standing there watching the fish. Now that's all it was, as I was no longer walking down the corridor to see my grandma. Each time I left, I would look back as I walked down the snake path, hoping to see a glimpse of my grandma's face and waving as always. I did this for a while, often being supported by Mrs Tutt. She used to stand with me, gazing into the pond watching the fish too, giving me company. I visited for a while, trying to find some solace. I had one tangible thing to hold on to, though. Grandma had left me the multi-coloured glass fish that I used to dust. I was so happy to have this passed down to me.

I regularly went with Mum and Dad to visit Grandma and Grandad's grave, placing fresh flowers and tidying the grave. On these visits, I would tell Grandma all the time how much I loved her and missed her dreadfully. These conversations became normal to me; it was the only way I could say what I wanted to say and hoped that she could hear me. I was lucky to have had my grandma in my life and will always hold the memories I have close to my heart. I never really felt like Grandma had gone far. I felt her by me most days. It's hard for me to explain; I just felt her presence. It wasn't until one night I realized my feelings had been right. She had not completely left us.

Each night from then on, my grandma would come and visit me as I lay down in my bed. I would feel her instantly; I knew it was Grandma. At first, I was frightened, but as I lay there, I would feel the gentlest touch on my head. This feeling was so loving that I no longer felt afraid. It was like she was stroking my head, making my body roll slightly as she sat alongside me on the edge of my bed. I told my parents a few times, but they never really responded. I'm not sure what they must have been thinking when hearing this. Maybe they just thought it was part of my grieving process, but this was not so. Her visitations came regularly, her presence and touch often aiding me to sleep. Sometimes I question myself as to why I felt no fear; I was a young girl. Even though this was my grandma that I adored, I was more than aware that she was no longer on this earth. Why was this becoming a normality for me?

Chapter 2

Moving On

With Mum working in the evenings and Dad working all hours, they needed to find someone to look after me. The obvious answer was to ask the next-door neighbours. We had always got on so very well with them and had lived next door to one another for years. The conversations over the fence were a daily occurrence, whether this was whilst Mum hung out the washing or simply coming back from shopping.

She was called Reeney and lived to the left of us with her husband Tom and their three children. They were a nice working-class family, making the best of what they had. Sharon was their eldest daughter, who promptly became my babysitter. Her babysitting skills worked well for a while. Little did she know that the events ahead would put her courage and bravery to the test.

Sharon used to come round at 5 pm, just in time for Mum to leave for work. We used to sit and watch television together or play eye spy. She was quite shy, with a slight nervousness about her. I liked her, though, and we seemed to interact well. Sometimes, Sharon would tell me what to do, and rightly so, being the one in charge. This didn't always go down well with me. I hated being told what to do, especially if I had other intentions in mind. Even as a child, I was always strong-headed.

On this one certain night, I remember having these strange feelings. I could tell that we weren't alone. I recognised the sensation as it was very similar to when Grandma visited me, although I instinctively knew that this was not her. At first, I attempted to shrug it off and started acting up because Sharon's mind was elsewhere, fully engrossed in a television show. Being the annoying child that I was, I started to stand in front of it, blocking her view. I knew this would get her attention. As I continued, she politely asked on a few occasions for me to move, but I insisted on staying exactly where I was.

Brimming with defiance and attitude, I looked straight at her and said, "There is someone outside the living room window."

It was dark by this time, so any visibility came from the flashing light of the beacon at the pedestrian crossing. Any access to the front of the house was via a small pathway that led past all the houses in our row. Sharon just looked at me, frowning.

"Don't be silly; no one is coming round," she said.

However, I was adamant that someone was standing right outside our living room window, and I continued on, telling her that there would be a knock on the window. A few seconds later, it happened.

Knock, knock.

Looking a little startled, Sharon got up and peered between the blind to see if she could see anyone there. No one was there. I started finding it funny and began laughing.

"They're going to knock again."

"Who are?" Sharon cautiously replied.

"I don't know exactly, but they are outside, and they're going to play with you."

And just as I spoke, came another bold knock on the window. I could see that Sharon was starting to feel a little uneasy now, but the same could not be said for me. I was enjoying this game; they were playful, and so was I. I told her to go to the door and see if she could see anything. This she did, but yet again, no one seemed to be there; well, not that she could see anyway.

A little while later, I began prancing around, Sharon continuously asking me to move out of the way of the television screen. So, I stood still and stared at her. As I did, the knocking started coming from the other side of the living room door. These knocks became louder and louder until Sharon jumped up from her chair.

"Stop banging on the door!" she shouted.

I sat down and stared at her. "It's not me."

She started to look scared, the colour slowly draining from her face until the banging finally stopped, but it wasn't over just yet. I told her to look at the door handle. As we both watched, the handle slowly started to move down; the room was now eerily silent. As it continued to go down, the door suddenly flew open and bashed against the wall. We both peered into the darkness of the hallway, but there was no one there. With that, Sharon quickly got up and slammed the door shut, kicking it with her foot. Within seconds, it flew open again. She started shouting at me as if I was doing it, but obviously, I wasn't. She kept saying stop it, over and over, her quivering voice starting to break.

"It's them," I said, "it's not me. They're just playing with you."

I looked over to Sharon; she sat there frozen, just her eyes moving back and forth towards the door.

Suddenly, the knocking returned, coming from the hallway. Each knock sounded more like a loud thud, vibrating the wall. This continued for quite a while, causing Sharon to get more upset with every passing minute. As the banging on the wall eased, the knocking on the window started again, and the lights in the living room began to flicker. That was the last straw; Sharon leapt from her chair and ran up to the bathroom, turning every light on as she went. She slammed the door shut and slid the small lock across. I sat at the top of the stairs waiting for her to appear, but she didn't. I soon realised that all the banging had come to a stop, and although I could still feel something with us, the game they had played was over.

Mum had arrived back from work; I could hear her voice from outside the window. I told her that Sharon had locked herself in the bathroom and wouldn't come out.

"Why on earth is she in there?"

Immediately, Mum could hear Sharon sniffling, so with a soft-spoken voice, she began talking to her through the door. After some time, Sharon appeared, looking traumatised and with noticeable red blotches around her eyes.

"I want to go home," she cried.

Mum asked Sharon what had happened this evening, and without hesitation, she pointed her finger in my direction, claiming it was all to do with me. Mum looked at me with a surprised look, and in that split moment, I wondered what she must have been thinking of me.

After Mum had seen Sharon home, she sat me down and asked what had gone on this evening. I simply shrugged my shoulders and replied.

"There were people here tonight, Mum; people you can't see. They were only playing games with her."

"What on earth are you talking about?" Mum said, looking bewildered. "Sharon was terribly upset this evening, so tomorrow, you will be apologising to her."

It seemed to me that my version of events had somehow got lost in translation and been brushed underneath the carpet.

The following day Reeney came round to have a chat with mum about the previous evening. I could hear Reeney saying how frightened and upset Sharon had been, and again, I was to blame. How was this the case? I had done nothing.

I apologised to Sharon. She never made any eye contact with me as I spoke to her. The only sure thing I knew was, she wasn't going to be babysitting me anymore. Later on, that day, I tried again to explain what had happened to Mum and Dad. Nothing that I said made any sense to them. I mean, where would I start? Would you believe me?

I saw Sharon a few times in passing. She acted so differently towards me now, very rarely staying long enough to speak more than a few words and still with very little eye contact. You could clearly see being in my company made her uncomfortable. I've never spoken about that night with her again; I think it's probably best not to. It was never my intention to cause her any emotional distress. I needed to learn to control my thoughts.

Chapter 3

Untapped Ability

As I grew up, like many young teenagers, I started battling with certain insecurities, such as the way I looked and how many friends I had. The anxiety all seemed to intensify in one place: school. Getting through each day was a struggle for me; I disliked school immensely.

Every morning I would walk up to the bus stop to wait for the school bus to arrive, meeting up with the same group of friends that lived on the estate. Naively, at this time of my life, education was of no importance to me. It's only when you get older that you realise the opportunities your schooling years could have given you. The monotony of starting every morning with your name being called out and being ticked off the register was never a good start for me, as I seemed to have a love-hate relationship with my registration teacher. She never tried hiding the fact that I was one of a few she disliked. I was always labelled as destructive and the one to lead my classmates astray. I pretty much got blamed for most things in class. By no means am I saying I was the perfect pupil, but I certainly wasn't to blame for most of what went on.

At this time of my life, I began to test the boundaries and started experiencing the trials and tribulations of growing up. One of the first was smoking. This I did with the same group of friends each time. The bell would ring, notifying us all that it was our break time. As soon as this was heard, a rush to get to the toilet block was on. We all squeezed into one cubicle, giggling and puffing away, the billowing smoke rising up and over the door. Now I'm not condoning smoking in any way, but to me, this was one of the reasons why I dragged myself out of bed every morning to go to school. The other motive for me going was I got on really well with my English and home economics teacher. I excelled in these classes.

I had a few close friends that I would spend most of my time with; one was called Gaby. Once school had finished for the day, we would walk around the local town centre and then make our way to her house. I also got on well with her mum. She was very friendly, always asking me if I wanted anything to eat or drink when we arrived. I noticed that she never seemed to stay for long, always busy doing something or going somewhere, but we didn't mind. This meant we had the house to ourselves.

One particular occasion is stuck forever, burning deep in my memory. It started with us both sitting in her living room, which was a fairly large size with two large leather sofas, an old wooden cabinet that stood underneath the bay window and a lovely open fireplace. We were talking about school and general teenage chatter when I noticed a familiar feeling in the atmosphere around me. Gaby knew nothing of my previous experiences, and I didn't really know what to do, so I tried to ignore it. The room was electric with waves of energy, and I soon realised that it was not going away. A presence was lingering right behind me; the tingling coldness had wrapped around my body. I couldn't keep quiet any longer.

"Do you believe in ghosts?" I asked jokingly.

To my surprise, Gaby said yes, and in a typical teenage manner, we started playing about, trying to scare one another. She was just about to tell me a creepy story when I suddenly felt this surge of strength and power around me. It grew ever stronger, the atmosphere pulsating as it moved about.

I glanced over to Gaby, and with no clear knowledge of what was to come next, I said, "Something is about to happen."

She pulled a funny face and shrugged her shoulders, not taking any notice. I knew by the bubbling feeling flowing through my body that I was right, and my focus instantly became fixed in the direction of her fireplace. I had no hesitation in expressing my belief that something was going to move the coal scuttle sitting on the hearth. Gaby looked over at me with a smirk across her face.

"What are you talking about? You've gone mad."

Why I had even thought this in the first place is beyond me. I just instinctively knew. Soon, the curious nature of Gaby got the better of her, and she started to encourage the situation. We stayed totally transfixed on it for a few minutes, waiting, until Gaby took in a sharp breath. The half-full coal scuttle slowly lifted from the hearth of the fireplace, hovered in the air, and after a few moments, dropped to the floor with a deafening thud. The sound rippled through me. Gaby clapped her hands over her ears, mouth wide open. We both stared at one another, in complete shock, not knowing whether to stay or run.

It seemed no time had passed when it began lifting again, slowly moving up in the air. This time, it changed direction and started floating to the centre of the room. It hovered for a short while suspended in midair, then abruptly fell to the floor, the nuggets of coal spilling across the rug. We were both completely dumbfounded. This time, we ran and headed straight for the stairs.

A sudden sound of howling wind swirled around the room, intensifying every minute, bursting out the doorway, chasing us. As quickly as we could, we flew up the stairs, Gaby in front of me. The sound of crashes and bangs followed us, thudding coming from the wall. I instinctively felt something or someone running closely behind me.

Gaby's bedroom was on the third floor of their townhouse, and by the time we reached the first-floor landing, one of the many pictures they had mounted on the wall fell to the floor, smashing into pieces. This was not to be the only one. As we continued up the stairs, every picture we passed flew off the wall. Both Gaby and I screamed at each one; we were so frightened by this stage. When we finally reached her room, we quickly looked behind us. The scene was from a horror movie; shattered glass and broken picture frames covered the floor.

As we entered Gaby's room, we slammed her bedroom door shut and jumped on her bed. We sat alongside one another, not saying a word, flinching at every noise that came from the other side of the door. To be honest, I wasn't sure what was going to happen next; this experience felt different to the others I had encountered.

Suddenly, the banging started coming from the other side of her bedroom door. It sounded as if something was being rammed against it, eager to hammer it down. We instantly put our arms around each other, hoping this would all stop, wishing the return of her mum. It continued for a while longer, which to us at the time seemed to go on endlessly.

We both let out a sigh of relief when her mum returned home. It was finally over. We both looked at one another as we opened her bedroom door. The look on our faces must have said it all.

"What the hell have you two been doing in here?" Gaby's mum boomed.

She looked so angry, and who could blame her? There were bits of wooden framing and shards of glass covering each step. How were we going to explain this? Where would we begin? We followed Gaby's mum into the kitchen, still not saying a word. As she turned to face us, we both started stuttering, trying our best to muddle through some kind of explanation as to what actually happened on that terrifying afternoon. The disbelief was written all over her face. She didn't believe us. We apologised continuously and promptly began to clear up the mess left behind from whatever it was that we encountered.

I stayed friends with Gaby all the way through school. We didn't really talk about what had happened much. It came up every now and again between us, but not to anyone else. We both knew that no one would believe us anyway, so what was the point? As we left school and got older, our friendship slowly dwindled. We saw each other in passing, but our journeys in life went in different directions. I often wonder what would have happened if Gaby's mum had been present in her house that day. She would have believed us then.

Chapter 4

Gypsy Lee

I was in my late teens when I met a charming young man, Steve. I was completely smitten and soon found myself falling head over heels for him. He was of similar age, tall and slender with bright blond hair. Our relationship grew from strength to strength, and thankfully, my parents enjoyed his company too, so he would often join us on family days out.

We always went out on a Sunday as that was Dad's day off, and Mum didn't drive. This particular Sunday was no different to any other. Mum and Dad came up with the idea that we all go down to the nearest seaside town for a walk along the shore. I agreed almost immediately, as we normally ended up getting a portion of chips. Mine were always drenched in vinegar, just how I like them. There was nothing like the aroma of takeaway chips at the seaside, the distinctive smell permanently wafting through the air. It makes my mouth water just thinking about it. The best was saved until last, though, and we always made a slight detour to the candy floss hut before our journey home, grabbing a bag of fluffy pink stuff. This always finished the trip off perfectly for me.

It only took us about an hour in the car, dependent on traffic. We parked up and walked along past the bumper cars and doughnut stall. It was a lovely day, dry and sunny with a light wind. As we approached the pier, we stopped by the nearest chippy and brought four bags of chips.

The pier had old fashioned penny drop machines and one-arm bandits; you couldn't go there without putting some pennies through the machines. The atmosphere, always bursting with bright lights and clinking noises, still gives me the same bubbling feelings of excitement in my tummy. Being there brought back many memories of when I was a little girl. Mum would lift me up every time, so I could place the pennies into the slot, then watch them cascade down to see if they would land in the right place, squealing with delight if any pennies dropped into my pot below.

A little further down from the amusements stood a lovely glass shop. You could see the owner through the shop window, blowing glass for the public to see. This often attracted crowds, and many stopped to watch.

As we began approaching the exit, I saw this little hut. It was painted in all the colours of the rainbow, with a sign saying palm reading. I was instantly intrigued to find out more and turned to Mum, asking her to come in with me. I don't think she was bothered to be honest, but she agreed to it anyway. This didn't interest my dad or Steve, so they went and sat down on a nearby bench and waited for us to come out. As Mum and I approached the doorway, a middle-aged lady opened the door. She had a paisley-coloured scarf on her head and wore a flowing dress with lots of silver bangles around both wrists that jangled with every movement she made.

"Can we come in?" I asked excitedly.

The lady looked at me sternly. "What are you doing here?"

I glanced over to Mum, shocked and confused with her greeting.

"I would like you to read my palm, please," I muttered, slightly anxious for her response.

"You can just carry on walking," she replied bluntly.

"I don't know who you think I am, but I think you're mixing me up with somebody else. This is the first time I've ever been here."

She raised both of her arms in the air and, with a big sigh, said, "Well, if you want to waste your money, then come on through."

Mum and I just simply looked at one another and shrugged our shoulders, clueless as to why this lady had such a problem. Thinking about it now, Mum and I should have just walked away. She was anything but welcoming, but we didn't and so proceeded to walk in and sit down on a couple of little stools with bright orange padded coverings.

As we sat on the opposite side of the table from the lady, Mum looked over to her and said, "You've totally got my daughter mixed up with somebody else."

Ignoring her, she cleared her throat and turned to face me. "Why don't you tell your mum all that she wants to know? You can tell her."

I was puzzled. What was this woman talking about? I remember thinking I should head for the exit and swiftly get out of there, but strangely, by this stage, I was too intrigued and wanted to know more. The lady couldn't seem to get comfortable, clearly agitated, wriggling around on her seat and often adjusting the tablecloth. Each silent second seemed to last forever until she let out another enormous sigh and dropped her hands heavily in her lap.

"I don't know why you have come here. Is it just to humour yourself by ridiculing me? You're well aware that you could be sitting here yourself."

Tutting, she roughly took my hand into hers and began reading my palm. Her dark brown eyes glazed over my hand, all the while the room stayed eerily still. I felt rather uncomfortable, to say the least; the whole experience to this point seemed so far from what I had imagined. The reading didn't last very long. As it came to an end, she looked up at me and abruptly released her grip from my hand, gesturing towards the door with her index finger.

"You can leave now. Don't come back".

It didn't take us long to walk out of there. We quickly placed the money on the table and made a fast exit. We were both pleased to leave and let out a sigh of relief the minute we got outside. As I glanced back, the woman was standing at the entrance of the hut, watching us walk away. The intense glare she gave felt like she was burning a hole in the back of our heads. There was no doubt in my mind that I would ever be returning.

When Mum and I caught back up with Dad and Steve, we

immediately started telling them both what had been said. Obviously, they were shocked to hear how adversely the lady had reacted to me being there. There was no real explanation for the palm reader's reaction. I simply put it down to a case of mistaken identity, but I will let you come to your own conclusion the further you read on. I must add that, over the years, I have become acquainted with a few palm readers and clairvoyants who have always been very pleasant and have shown copious amounts of wisdom in their profession.

Chapter 5

Night Visitations

It was becoming clear to me that receiving nightly visitations from the spirit world was part of my life, of who I was. This made me feel different from many of the people I was close to. I felt alone. Why was it that I could feel spirits and hear them talking, and no one around me could do the same?

Most evenings, Steve would ride down on his bicycle from his house to mine. We would spend hours walking, holding hands and chatting about what we had been up to that day. We valued our time together, and our relationship soon flourished. Steve, at this point, was unaware of my experiences with the paranormal. It wasn't something you would naturally discuss. I was worried to do so in case he started looking at me in a different way. Most nights, as Steve left to go home, I would rush up to my bedroom and stand at my window to say goodnight to him. We would wave continuously to one another as he cycled up the road until he was out of sight.

More often than not, I would be standing at my bedroom window when the atmosphere immediately started to shift. I would feel the temperature start to drop, along with the pressure in the air. My ears buzzed. By the time I had gone into the bathroom to brush my teeth, a spirit was felt. I could sense them standing at the bathroom doorway, or sometimes right behind me, an unnerving chill running through my body.

My bedroom was situated at the rear of the house, and as soon as it got dusk, all the streetlights would come on with a warm orange glow. Once Mum and Dad had gone to bed and turned all the lights off, the house was pitch black apart from my bedroom. The streetlights radiated through my curtains, softly lighting up my room. Being able to see a little at night gave me some comfort.

Once I had been lying in bed for a short while, I would begin noticing a cold air blowing over my face, accompanied by noises. When I say noises, it's more like distant rustling, similar to hearing someone walk on the carpet in their slippers, dragging their feet. I could follow the noise and pretty much pinpoint whereabouts they were standing every time. At this stage, I didn't often see the apparitions, although this made no difference to me at all. There was never any disputing that they were there.

At times, I would get an intense feeling inside my head. A heavy pressure, pushing down like my head was in a vice, the whole circumference getting tighter and tighter. Loud buzzing noises, deep within my ears. It wasn't always a pleasant feeling, but one I became accustomed to.

There often seemed to be more than one energy circulating, and this normally happened after my grandma had visited. Some of the spirits would only stay at the entrance of my door, just looking in, not venturing past the architrave. The loose floorboard at the entrance of my doorway creaked without fail with any weight or pressure placed on it, a sure sign that someone was there. Others had no problem with crossing the threshold and came in.

The intensity in my room would build, a forceful whirlwind circulated, and misty hazes would start to gradually manifest. They appeared in mid-air, like small areas of smoke that was beginning to separate. I would hear objects on top of my wardrobe rustling, movement of the wardrobe doors. There was thudding against my bed, strong enough to make my body move. Pressure occurred on the bed covers, and soft whispers travelled through the air, though not clear enough for me to decipher. Their whispers sound as though they're standing right by me, but also so far away. There's a distance to their calls - an echoing from afar, even though I felt them close by.

The energies always felt stronger at the beginning of the night, but as time ticked by, I would feel the powerful atmosphere diminish and clear. Spirit activity would begin to lessen, the pressure in my head would ease, and their need for contact drifted away. The more this happened, the more I was able to begin to settle myself down, ready to sleep. However, sleeping on this one particular night was not something that came easily.

Chapter 6

Turning Point

I had started to notice a change in spirit contact. The usual energies seemed the same, but there was something else happening. Around this period, I realised that everything my parents and the church had spoken about regarding heaven and hell was becoming more and more of a reality. This one terrifying night was the turning point. I encountered an entity of pure evil, filled with nothing but darkness and negativity. She became the first of many from that moment on, where I started to see spirits clearly.

Most evenings started off with me feeling the presence of spirits circulating my room, but this time, the whole atmosphere felt off to me. Something was looming. My body kept shuddering, goose pimples popping up all over me. As I lay there in my bed, I began hearing a strange sound. It was an eerie whistling sound, like someone was trying to call me and catch my attention. The whistling seemed like it was coming from the corner of my room, in the gap between my wardrobe and the bedroom door.

I was being drawn to look at it. A forceful pull I had not felt before. My gut was screaming at me, telling me not to look and to just run away, but I couldn't stop. As it continued, I sat myself up, thankful for the streetlights that brought a glow into certain areas of my room. The more my eyes focused, the more I was able to see the outline of a crouching figure slowly emerging from the darkness.

I started to tremble. My heart was pounding in my chest. The face of an elderly lady was looking back at me. Her sharp features edged more out of the shadows and into the light. The harsh, jagged edges to her face were framed by thin, wispy silver hair, and her beady eyes seemed to burn right through me. She just kept staring, with no expression at all.

I wanted to shout out to Mum, but for some reason, I was unable to. The words seemed stuck in my throat. I gradually pulled the quilt up under my chin, holding on to it so tightly that my fingers started to lock. Suddenly, she began to laugh continuously. It was just like a witching cackle, something you'd hear in a nightmare. The haunting sound still resonates with me today.

"You're a stupid, stupid girl," She sniggered, repeating it over and over.

Her dark intent emanated from within, filling the air with grossness. The fear that I felt was overwhelming.

I squeezed my eyes shut and finally got the courage to shout out for Mum. I nervously opened them, praying that the lady would be gone. She was still there, a malevolent smirk upon her face. Finally, I heard familiar footsteps coming from the hallway, and like a shining, bright beacon of hope, Mum appeared. She fumbled around for the light switch, half asleep and flicked it on.

"What's wrong?" she said, rubbing her eyes.

I glanced over to the corner. She was gone. I felt my body instantly relax, and I let out an enormous sigh of relief.

"I had a terrible dream," I muttered, knowing deep down that this was a lie. I couldn't bring myself to tell her the truth. To try and explain seemed too difficult; I was still coming to terms with it all myself.

Before Mum went back to bed, she came over and sat with me and gave me a comforting cuddle, assuring me that everything would be ok. The feeling of Mum wrapping her arms around me gave me a warm sense of security. I didn't really want her to go. My bedroom light stayed on for the rest of that night, in fear that I would see that horrible face.

I told myself over and over again that more often than not, good overpowers the bad. With much relief, that lady did not return, and to this day, I haven't seen or heard from her again. Unfortunately, little did I realise that this would not be the last of this kind of visitation.

Chapter 7

Dark Senses

Some time had passed, and I had been in a relationship with Steve for a number of years. Lust grew to love so naturally; the more we saw each other, our connection became stronger each day. To enable us some time alone, we would often take ourselves off for a walk to a lovely woodland nearby, which opened out onto a clearing that often had cricket matches played on. We would walk for hours, talking about all sorts of things, laughing and enjoying every bit of each other's company.

One chilly Sunday, whilst enjoying the walk, I started to open up about the paranormal events that I was experiencing. To this day, I'm not sure where the sudden surge of courage came from, but I didn't like the thought of keeping things from him, and the time just felt right. It was now or never. I approached the subject cautiously and waited to see how he would respond. As the conversation went on, I found myself feeling at ease talking about it. Steve seemed fine, even though I could see this wasn't something he had had any dealings with before. He was honest enough to say he found the subject unnerving and didn't understand the reality of it all. I completely understood his confusion. I was just grateful that he listened to me without judgement and didn't want to leave.

I was pleased to have opened up about most of my experiences, and I felt a slight release in sharing my troubles with someone closest to me. As they say, a problem shared is a problem halved. I thought it unnecessary to speak about the unpleasant visitations that I had recently had and felt that everything I had already told him was enough for one day.

Unfortunately, it was a time in my life where it didn't matter what time of the day it was; strange things just started happening. The phrase 'seeing is believing' was about to test Steve to new heights, whether he liked it or not. His world of unbelievable was about to become entirely believable.

We had been out for a leisurely walk and decided to relax on the sofa to watch an afternoon film. We were happily cuddled up together enjoying Cocoon, one of my favourite movies, when I noticed Mum and Dad's hanging plant that hung down from the ceiling had started moving. At first, I chose to ignore it, hoping that with no acknowledgement, it would stop. It wasn't long before this had caught Steve's eye, his attention being diverted over in that direction too. The initial, small circling movements now led to an unmistakable motion. There was no reason for the pot to have started moving at all, let alone moving in the way it was. There were no windows or doors open at the time that could have caused a draft.

We both looked at one another, not saying a word, just watching, eyes wide open. As we continued to stare, the movements of the pot became stronger. It started spinning erratically, round to the left, then to the right, then swaying from side to side like a boat on rough seas. I could see from Steve's expression that he was uncertain as to what he was witnessing. He got up from the sofa and went over to investigate. Reaching up to the pot, he cupped it in his hands, bringing it to a sudden stop. He stood there for a short while, with a glazed stare, his expression perplexed. It wasn't long before it began again. This time, it was swaying from side to side with such force that it was only millimetres away from hitting the ceiling.

"This is what they do," I whispered, looking over to Steve.

All of a sudden, the pot came to a sharp standstill. It was as if Steve had stopped it again with his hands, but this time he hadn't touched it. Neither of us said a word. As we sat in silence, the lace net curtains to my parent's porch began to move, catching my eye. The net slowly began lifting up and out towards the middle of the room. It was like someone was walking underneath it, brushing over their head then gradually falling down. Similar in fact to when I was a little girl, pretending that I was getting married, walking underneath the netting like it was the veil on my wedding gown.

This was more than enough for Steve to witness for the first time. I can remember how terrified I was back then, and I felt for him immensely. He looked awfully uncomfortable with the experience and was visibly anxious to leave. Even so, he stayed, and we discussed it together for a while, realising quickly that no matter how much we spoke about it, the conclusion was always the same. There was no plausible reason for what had happened.

It was a relief to see Steve the following evening. We took a stroll down to the old railway line, which ran along the bottom of the housing estate. We perched on the brick wall, admiring the night's sky that was filled with twinkling stars, like diamonds. It felt like the perfect evening, the air of the night was warm, and the wind was still. We snuggled up close, holding hands and showering each other with affection like love-struck teenagers. Little did we know how quickly the calmness of the night could turn into a raging storm.

Whilst enjoying the attention we were giving one another, I started to sense an ominous presence lurking around us. This was unusual for me, as I had not experienced many spirits outside my house. Doing my best to ignore it, I began to feel agitated, with an overwhelming ball of anger building deep inside of me. It surged through my veins. I could feel it from the tip of my toes, right up to the top of my head. The more I tried to resist and push it to the back of my mind, the stronger it seemed to take hold. I didn't know what to do.

I looked at Steve and said that I wasn't feeling great and thought it best that we went back to mine. As soon as I said this, a howling wind began to circle around us. It came from nowhere. The immense strength of the wind mirrored a powerful hurricane. I knew this was no natural occurrence. Until now, the only breeze we had felt was light and warm.

I wanted to turn my back and leave, but I couldn't. We could hear the trees straight in front of us start to creak as the wind began to swirl between them. It seemed to build energy with every passing moment. They swayed so violently. As we looked along the railway embankment, we could see that none of the surrounding trees were moving at all. There was hardly a breeze in the air where they stood. We became fixated with how it was possible that only the few trees straight ahead of us were moving in such a way. It was obvious to us that we were witnessing something strange, unimaginable and very eerie.

The air around us gradually became still, back to the same lightness as before. However, I continued to feel this ball of energy pulsing through my body. A feeling of undeniable rage was building up inside, overtaking my thoughts. This was overwhelming; the intent to hurt someone or something was so strong. This was not me at all. I hadn't and never would intentionally hurt anyone or anything. With an urgency to my voice, I told Steve that we needed to leave; otherwise, I felt I would possibly do something to him that I would deeply regret.

As we swiftly departed the area, the intense anger soon turned into terror. I knew then at that point I was capable of just about anything and nothing of good intent. It was extremely alarming to feel as though I had no control of my own actions. It was becoming apparent that the intensity and strength of this dark energy force was becoming too much for me to ignore. For reasons unknown, it seemed to be tracking me down, watching my every move. I felt scared and extremely vulnerable.

Unfortunately for Steve, he had now witnessed one of the terrifying events with his own eyes and would hopefully now find a place of some understanding. Understanding of what I was up against. I held my fear close to my chest, with an overwhelming uncertainty looming over me all the time.

I didn't mention any of the issues Steve and I had witnessed that evening to Mum and Dad. It was so unfathomable and far-fetched that I thought it was best to be left between the two of us.

Chapter 8

The Witnessing

I hadn't felt the malicious energy during the day since the episode with my parent's plant pot. Needless to say, they made up for it come night-time. I had begun praying to the Lord, asking for his guidance. This gave me the feeling that I was not alone with these evil entities. By now, I could recognise the intense sense of darkness they brought with them. It overwhelmed me. A dampened dark blanket, consuming me with negativity. I felt they did this as a form of intimidation, hoping to weaken every ounce of strength I had. They hungered after my fear with each visit and fed from this every time. It was like I gave them strength with every weakness I showed.

Night-time brought a deep fear for me, along with apprehension, weakness and self-doubt. Every conceivable negative word you could pick from a dictionary filled me from the inside out. As I lay in my bed this one memorable night, I'd anxiously await the next stage. The room was full of echoes, of unexplainable noises. The new, noticeable smell of burning tobacco filled my nose. The aroma was unpleasant. It came with damp, suffocating air. It shrouded the room. My mind became completely focused on the activities surrounding me. The power behind the presence couldn't and wouldn't be ignored.

The familiar glow from the streetlights shone through my curtains, giving me some welcomed light from the dark. This was only for a short while. I began to notice a black formation appearing at the bottom of my bed. It was like a floating, thick, black blanket rising from the floor, remaining static for a short time, before slowly edging closer and closer towards me, leaving behind a trail of dullness as it continued to move up my body and over my head. By now, I was unable to see any illumination of the streetlights entering my room. It engulfed me; I could see nothing at all, not even my hand in front of my face. I could hear the presence circling the room, brushing itself along the walls and ceiling.

As time ticked away, the mass of what I called 'the black blanket' started breaking down. I could see the consistency of it beginning to thin, resembling ink. As it continued to break down, I was able to see the subtle light coming back in. With the presence still dominating my room, my gaze became drawn to where there was a small chair. It had many items of my clothing scattered over it. My eyes were transfixed. I could hear distinctive, rustling sounds coming from that direction. At the top of the chair, I was able to make out an image of the same dark mist formation. The harder I looked, the more I could see two eyes peering over the top of the chair at me. It took my breath away immediately. They were a burning orange colour in an oval shape, resembling cat's eyes. It soon became apparent that more than just one pair of eyes were looking over at me from behind the chair: some were piercing bright green, others burning orange and red. The intensity of their stare felt like they were boring into my soul.

I desperately wanted to look away, but felt I was unable to do so - like I was under some kind of spell. These eyes were peering everywhere around the chair. They appeared along the armrests, along the top and looking from underneath it. They had a strong presence of evil omitting from them. I could feel it in the pit of my stomach. They held bad intentions from within, coming from a dwelling far down in the earth's core. I was crushed inside with fear. I didn't know what to do, but with a nudge of guidance from my own subconscious, I placed my hands together and prayed. I repeated myself over and over, asking the Lord to surround me with his love and light, to protect myself and my family from the evil that was around us. I have no words to describe the real fear I was experiencing. I could do nothing more but to huddle under the safety of the quilt, gripping it tightly, hoping that it would all go away.

The activity continued into the early hours, then slowly subsided. I could tell instantly when they had begun to disperse because the room would feel lighter. The smell of burning tobacco smoke would disappear, leaving the atmosphere in my room calm once again.

After managing to capture a few hours of sleep, I woke up, still feeling the lingering, negative residue from the occurrences that had happened only hours ago. It was then that I came to the conclusion I needed to see if others were able to feel and hear these paranormal activities too. This would be reassuring both for my own sanity and also to have someone else witness these events. The thing is, I wouldn't be able to say anything to this person about what they are likely to experience during their night stay, or this would be in their expectations. It could mean they wouldn't be so willing to stay with me after all.

I felt apprehensive about doing this. Putting someone innocently into an experience of the unknown would be very frightening for them, but it really was the only way forward. It sounds like an unkind thing to do to someone, but I needed this validation. I wanted to know that I wasn't the only one who could hear and see these entities. It was time to no longer fear the night alone. I needed all the support I could find.

I made the decision to invite a close family member to stay over with me. She was a great choice; we had a good relationship and was pretty much the same age. I knew the invitation would be accepted easily; we often spent time together, and she enjoyed the company of my mum and dad too.

Running up to the following weekend, I invited Grace over to stay. We spent the whole day together, mainly lazing around on the sofa watching films. That same evening, Mum and Dad brought us all a takeaway. We decided to take our meal up to my room to enjoy whilst listening to the Top 40 charts. We talked nonstop for hours. Gossiping, giggling, having fun. Time had soon passed. I could hear Mum and

Dad making their way upstairs to go to bed. Mum popped her head around the door and suggested we get ready for bed and start settling down as it was getting late.

Grace was sleeping in my bed, and I had the comfort of the floor in my sleeping bag. We snuggled down and continued our chit chat for a little while longer. After a short time, we both began to feel tired and decided to call it a night.

As the room became quiet, I wondered if the presence would come at all. Would it act differently, seeing as there was someone else in my room with me tonight? I didn't have to wait long to have my question answered. The same black mist had started to form, hovering just above the floor. It flowed outwards, spreading to both sides of the room. Slowly with time, I watched this formation grow bigger and bigger until it smothered every inch of my room. It seemed to move continuously within itself, like mist rolling over mountain peaks. As I lay motionless in my sleeping bag, the feeling of tension mounting in my body was undeniable. I could feel my heart pounding. The atmospherics in my room began changing as usual, with the air becoming suppressed.

I wasn't sure at this point if Grace was awake or not, so I gently spoke out to her and asked.

She replied, her voice quivering, "What are all those noises?"

I paused for a few seconds before answering. "I don't know. What noises?"

I felt mean in so many ways, keeping everything from her, but it was the only way to see if Grace could also see and hear what was happening around us. As I lay there, I started hearing the same clicking noises as the previous nights. They were faint at first but soon loud enough to be heard clearly. It sounded like the crackling off a firework.

By this stage, Grace had become frightened with the unfolding activities. She promptly asked me to join her in the bed, which I did. We lay side by side, holding hands, comforting one another. I could feel something was right beside me. I felt a heavy breath on my face. The weight of the air against my skin made my toes curl. I turned my face closer towards Grace, trying to be as far away as possible from this unknown force.

Within seconds, I felt it touch me. It was a feeling of being pricked many times with hot needles. The intense static noise was echoing against my ear. It was like the static heard when separating clothes that had just been tumble dried. I could feel the beads of sweat lubricating the palms of my hands with fear. All of a sudden, Grace started flapping her arms about, crying.

"Something's touching me. I can feel something touching me," she screamed.

I couldn't put her through any more of this. Enough was enough. I built up some courage, and jumped out of bed and turned the light on. Grace was sobbing her heart out. I put my arms around her and tried to comfort her as much as I could. Even with the light on, the static clicking noise around the ceiling could still be heard.

For Grace's own mental state, I suggested that we leave my bedroom and go downstairs. You could blatantly see how shook up she was; her whole body was shaking. Still sobbing, she kept asking me about everything that went on in my room. I never did answer her fully. With all the commotion we were making downstairs, Mum soon came down, wanting to know what was going on. With the best will in the world, Grace tried to explain everything to mum. Mum's face said a thousand words; she didn't really need to say anything.

After a few sips of a hot cup of tea, Grace finally stopped crying and seemed a little more settled, although she insisted that she wanted to go home. Mum went upstairs to get Dad out of his bed and asked him to take her back home.

After Grace had left my house, it seemed to me that there was no better time than now to sit down and speak to Mum about everything I had been experiencing. I didn't expect mum to believe all that I was saying to her. I did ask, though, for Mum to stay in my room for a night and see for herself what I had been enduring of late as each night emerges.

Chapter 9

They Finally See

Mum and I continued to speak about my spiritual experiences. I left no stone unturned. I brought up the most recent episodes I had been having, along with my reasoning for bringing Grace into the situation. I could tell Mum was doing her best to understand and take in all I was saying, trying to put the information into some context that made any sense. The general look of concern and uncertainty was etched on her face.

Having talked everything through, I found a sense of comfort within myself. This was simply a sense of relief. I had unburdened all this paranormal baggage that had been circling inside my mind for such a long time. It felt good to have the support from my parents; it was like forming a band of unity on my side. Even though I know they found it a challenging concept to grasp and to comprehend.

As our conversation ended, mum decided that she would stay with me that night.

"No time like the present," she said hesitantly, raising her eyebrows.

Inside I felt elated; I was so pleased that finally, Mum would see it for herself. No greater time for the proverb; seeing is believing. This should settle the matter once and for all. If it didn't, at least I had her with me for company, and I wouldn't be scared alone.

It was getting on for 11.15 pm, so I went up and got myself ready for bed. After a short while, mum joined me. We both settled down, the feeling of apprehension paramount. What would this night bring?

We talked about how Dad always made-up excuses for the noises I used to mention in the early days of my experiences. It was always either the pipes in the house were cooling down, or the central heating was making the wood expand, and so it went on.

As we lay there, the same atmospheric changes in the air could be felt. The strong rancid smell of burning, stale cigarette aroma filled the room. Then, as with previous nights, came the black blanket formation. Yet again filling the whole room, submerging us into complete darkness. Now I couldn't see Mum, and she couldn't see me. I wiggled myself as close as I could next to Mum and interlocked our arms for added security. I always seemed to become extremely agitated from this point on, with a dreaded feeling overriding every cell of my body.

I could sense Mum's apprehension; the muscles in her arms twitched and clenched. With all the negativity that I had been experiencing lately, I felt the need to own a crucifix of Jesus or a statue of The Virgin Mary - anything religious to have beside me each night. So, I had visited our local catholic church, which was based on the outskirts of our local town. There I found a beautiful large crucifix with Jesus mounted on the cross. After purchasing, the resident priest kindly blessed it for me, which gave me this extraordinary sense of security. Once I got home, the first agenda was to hang this up straight away. I fixed it into the ceiling, allowing the crucifix to hang freely, positioned just above my head as I slept.

As the atmosphere in my room grew ever stronger, I kept the image of my crucifix firmly in my mind eye, praying for our protection from this essence of evil circulating my room. The loud clicking of static electricity began travelling around the edges of the ceiling again. The whirling wind was howling past our ears. Suddenly, I felt mum's hand squeezing my arm.

With a whisper, she said, "I can hear it."

Hearing those four words made me so emotional. It was an enormous sense of relief having my mum witness it too. Now, I knew for certain I would never have to live in fear again. Mum would help me, give me the love and support I needed.

The constant clicking seemed louder and more prominent than usual. The speed at which it travelled around the perimeter of the ceiling made me more than aware that this was building up to something. The air felt so thick; it made taking a breath harder to do. A forceful wind started circulating us, bringing in new noises. A growling. A deep, rumbling sound that made me want to scream with sheer terror.

"I can hear that too. What is that?" Mum said, her voice getting louder and sterner.

I didn't answer; I just buried my head in her shoulder. The mini cyclone continued to whirl around my room. It bounced to and fro from each wall as it travelled erratically round and round. The pressure within my room began hurting our ears deep down inside. It was like an intense earache pounding the eardrum. Every now and again, we could feel the quilt being pulled. With each alarming tug, we flinched, dreading the next. With all the chaos surrounding us, Mum sat upright in bed, looking all over the place in every direction, trying to figure out what was happening.

She gasped. "Lovie, do you feel that too?"

I gulped, and my body instantly tensed up. "Yes, Mum. I think someone is on the bed."

It was very clear that something was on the bed with us. We were able to pinpoint each indentation being made as it slowly moved up the bed towards us. It felt similar to the pressure a cat makes as it prowls over the top of your quilt. It got up to around my stomach and then thankfully stopped.

We still couldn't see a thing, not even our hands in front of our faces. It was pitch black. All that was noticeable at this point was a small, flickering orange object that started to appear in one corner of the ceiling. It looked like a small flame, waving out from the crevice - the same size as you would see when using a lighter. Then, in the blink of an eye, once we had seen one, more and more of these small flickering flames appeared, eventually covering the perimeter of the ceiling. The clicking sounds coincided with every flame. The rancid smell still lingered in the air; every breath we took burnt our noses and filled our throats.

Even though the wind continued to hurl around the room, the fire never went out. With our hearts rapidly pounding within our chests, it felt difficult to concentrate. All the time, we were trying to control the surges of fear pulsating through our bodies. Every inch of us was channelling the fight and flight response.

The growling started up again. It was clear but weirdly had an echoing tone to it as though it was coming from a distance. It was deep, with an eerie undertone to it. This noise, moving ever closer, filled our heads with a deep rumbling tone, like thunder bouncing along the sky. The vibrations rattling our brains within our skulls.

I began grasping the bottom sheet tightly. The distinctive sound of something brushing alongside the wall beside me was plain enough for me to hear. As it reached me, I could feel it gliding over every inch of my body, circulating underneath my back and wrapping me within its grasp. I was absolutely terrified, completely frozen with fear. I tried so hard to get Mum's attention by uttering a sound, but was incapable of doing so. I continued to endure the stench of its breaths against my face, releasing stagnant air all over my skin. I could feel a force of energy pulling me towards it. It was trying all the more to engulf me with its traits of evil. My body started shaking. I began feeling a strong surge entering through my body; it was taking over me. It was as if I was in a trance, in a different time and place. I had lost control of my mind and body. I was being controlled.

Time slipped by. I could feel mum vigorously shaking me, shouting my name again and again. I heard her panicked calls but was unable to reply. In a flick of a switch, the whole situation took an unbelievable turn of events. I can only tell you what happened next through Mum's memories, as I have no recollection at all.

This entity continued in its attempts to encapsulate me. To peel me away from my happy life to its underworld. Knowing quite how long this all went on for is hard to say exactly, but it had taken some ongoing efforts from Mum to bring me around from the trance-like state that I was being held in. Mum said she continued to shout at me, shake me, try to bring me back. The last moment of this horrific night was noticing that my bedroom light was on. I can remember not being able to see it clearly; the brightness of the bulb shone like a shimmering haze. I continuously rubbed my eyes in the hope of clearing my vision.

After doing this, I turned to acknowledge Mum, and it became apparent to me by the look on her face that something other than what we had both experienced that night had happened. Mum's normal peachy complexion looked so pale, as white as a ghost. Horrified by what she had seen, Mum retrieved Dad from his bed. With a wobbling uncertainty in her voice, Mum started to explain everything. A cluster of flames from the ceiling had sectioned off and began travelling along to above my bed, where my crucifix was positioned. The cluster continued to travel down the rope that held it suspended in the air. As it got closer to the crucifix, the individual flames started bouncing back and forth erratically. The crackling sounds seemed louder as they moved endlessly around the outline of the cross. It was as if the energy was trying to enforce its power over the protection and strength that the crucifix was omitting but to no avail.

As Mum watched this, she noticed a glowing colour of luminous green from the corner of her eye. It wasn't until Mum looked properly over in my direction that she realised in horror, the glowing of green was coming from my eyes. With some hesitancy, she continued to explain that this glow of luminous green covered my entire eye and radiated outwards towards the end of my nose. My eyes were in a fixed state, with no blinking or moving. Frozen with every imaginable feeling of fear and disbelief, Mum found her thoughts and reactions numbed to such a degree that for a short while, she felt unable to do anything to try and help me.

As I came round from this trance-like state, I noticed Dad sitting beside Mum on the bed. He looked like a fish out of water. His mouth was open with a dead blank stare, but he tried to listen intently to Mum's recollections of the night. I know to this present day that he found all that was said to him just too much to comprehend. The realisation that this was all real and happening within the walls of his home sent his thoughts to places they'd never been before. I can truly understand the hardship my dad had with it all. This was a situation that Dad had no control over. For the first time ever, he was unable to ward this problem away from me. Unable to shield and protect his youngest daughter, as he always has done.

On the other hand, Mum had now seen this dark manifestation for herself. Understandably terrified, as was I, she found the strength to stand by me through this night, witnessing unimaginable visions that can only ever truly be believed when you've seen them with your own eyes.

It had become apparent to us all that this diabolical evil had found its time to fully show what it was made of. Its intentions had become clear. My days had become consumed with terror, thoughts of the night ahead, and to what the coming night would bring forth. The ongoing fear was still destroying my life. I felt a difference in the way I handled myself in daily situations. Normally a strong, fun-loving individual, I was now uncertain, scared and unbalanced: half of the personality I once had. I know I had an air about me that seemed flippant to everyone and everything around me, with an anger inside that consistently simmered under my skin. It had taken such a toll on me, physically and mentally. I was so tired of being terrorised by this entity, night after night. I was worn with its ongoing luring, which had eaten up most of the strength I had. I felt like I was losing a grip of my own soul.

The time had finally come. My parents had been in touch with our resident vicar from our local church, Reverend Francis, requesting his company at our home to discuss what I had been experiencing. I had met Francis many times previously. We often stood and spoke for a short while after Sunday service. That was when I had time to attend. He was always genuine in nature, with no airs or graces about him, generally a pleasant man of the church.

On the evening that Francis was due to arrive, I found myself in a ball of nerves. This was more than likely down to the nature of the conversation I was about to have with him. How will he receive this information, and more importantly, what help can I hope to receive? I didn't have long mulling over my thoughts before Francis knocked at the door. I was so pleased to see him. He shook my hand and sat down with me in the living room. Both of my parents also sat in on the conversation, as it was important that he also heard their accounts of what they had witnessed.

As Francis sipped away at his cup of tea, I began to unfold all the details regarding the experiences I'd had, starting from way back, through to when I was a child, and then to the present day's situation. It must have sounded like a lengthy tale, one that years ago would have had me burnt at the stake for showing witch-like tendencies.

Surprisingly, by the time I had finished my life memoirs of the past years to him, he simply replied with, "I know just the person that can help us stand together to banish this monstrosity."

His voice was strong, bold. He instantly filled me with confidence and hope. He continued to say that another reverend he knew very well had become known for helping such individuals as myself from these parasites that trouble us. Francis explained that, unfortunately, it might take a week or two for John, the other reverend, to be free to meet us, as he's a busy man with his work. Those words horrified me at first, the thought of yet another couple of weeks. Thankfully, with every ounce of gratitude, this was not the case for me. After Francis had explained everything to him later that day, Reverend John was more than happy to cancel a couple of bookings to come and meet me as soon as possible. I was overjoyed in hearing this. He couldn't come quick enough.

The days seemed to drag longer than usual, but those few nights were just slightly easier to bear, knowing in the back of my mind that help was hopefully not too far away.

Whilst waiting for Reverend John to arrive, my anticipation grew greater as the minutes passed. He would be here any second. I heard the back gate click shut and then a few knocks. My heart began pounding in my chest. As I opened the door, there stood a large-statured man, carrying a warm smile on his face. He was dressed in black trousers and a black shirt, with his white clerical collar ever so prominent. From the moment he cupped my hands in his, I felt a sense of strength, not just from his grip but radiating from him. I led him through to our living room. We all sat down and discussed the present issues that were troubling my daily life.

As I spoke, I felt his interest in every word that left my mouth, which gave me a sense of his understanding of what I was saying. No matter how far out and unbelievable it may have seemed, his acknowledgement of my plight was paramount. After I had told him all that he needed to know, John sat and asked me some questions too. He started by asking if there were any objects that I knew of within the house that possibly represented the devil in any way. Neither I nor my parents had or would ever have purchased such goods, but my older brother, on the other hand, had been an avid antique collector for years. He often brought home all sorts of items that he had purchased. He left some of them behind prior to leaving the family home to make a life for himself in London. These such items had been boxed up and left in the attic until a time of convenience that enabled my brother to collect them and take them back to his new property. Reverend John requested to look at all of these. He continued to say that sometimes, such items can hold a negative residue from past events.

My dad retrieved the boxes from the attic and placed them down, allowing Reverend John to begin rifling through these objects. Amongst the many items, some were beautiful ornaments, and he noticed a large bubble wrapped ornament. It used to take pride of place on my brothers' chest of draws in his bedroom. The ornament in question was a large, cream adaptation of Pan, symbolising a figure of half-man, half-goat from Greek mythology. This did not please

Reverend John at all. He requested the immediate destruction of this ornament to my parents, explaining that, within the realms of Christianity, Pan is looked upon as a form of demonic representation. Pan has the hindquarters and horns of a goat, in the same manner as a faun or satyr.

As alarming as this sounded to them both, my parents declined any participation in the destruction of this particular ornament. This was my brother's property and something he would have saved long and hard to purchase. However, seeing the distasteful look on Reverend John's face, they agreed that such an item should not be in the house and would make prompt arrangements for my brother to remove it.

As the evening went on, Reverend John wanted to see my bedroom, this being the main area in the house that the issues were arising from. We all entered my room. Reverend John stood there, silent, yet with a dominating presence. He turned to us and explained that he was feeling for any atmospheric changes in the air from paranormal residue. Neither of us moved a muscle or uttered a sound. We stood stuck to the floor, watching him in awe. After a short time, he suggested that we stand together, holding one another's hands. As we did this, the reverend began to recite the Lord's Prayer.

With no other words spoken, we returned to the lounge area to continue our discussion. As we sat down, Reverend John said that he had indeed felt a strong sense of a dark presence within my room. He went on to say that these menacing entities come, attempting to seduce you. With many years of experience, I have been one of the many young females of a certain age that he has come across experiencing the same intrusion. Reverend Johns words continued; these satanic entities single out young women like you in a bid to overrule your thought process. This is in the hope that you will succumb to Satan's way and spread the word of his work, in turn, becoming a soldier within his army of sin. Good and evil fill this world, both physically as well as the outer realms.

In hearing these words from a holy man, I felt my knees buckle from underneath me. I was completely overwhelmed. I felt sick to my stomach; the thought of what he was saying seemed unreal. Only in fiction books and movie plots do you see these horror situations played out. This was my life. No re-enactments or clever simulations. For me, most of what was said after that statement from Reverend John became a blur, to be honest. However, his distinctive, deep, bellowing voice suggesting action should be taken immediately to banish this unholy presence from our home was clearly heard. With my dwindling mental state apparent, it was set. Reverend John would return with some of his colleagues tomorrow evening to perform an exorcism.

The feeling of hope filled my soul. Will I at long last be rid of these nights of torment? As hopeful as I was, I still had a niggling uncertainty about it. I mean, I had seen these rituals performed on television before, but never standing present. With my already wired mind, thoughts started racing. Could this exorcism ritual cause the entity to become enraged, making my current situation all the more of a problem than it already is? I knew I needed to settle myself down, stop the negative thoughts and go forward with a positive notion. This could be the answer to everything: the resolution.

I heard Mum and Dad discuss the prospect for most of the night, reflecting their hopes and prayers that this was the light at the end of the tunnel for all of us. As bedtime approached, the normality of my night-time terror awaited as usual. This time, though, could be the last, which filled me with all the fighting spirit I required to get me through another night.

The later it became, the more intrusive the entity would be. The continual touches to my face, the same intense atmospherics, like a pressure squeezing within the ceiling and walls as they begin to close in around me. The same strong sense of being mentally manipulated and engulfed within an air that suffocated my room. I was forever trying to occupy my own thoughts from the never-ending invasion of the darkness surrounding me.

I began silently chanting four keywords over and over again; *I must stay strong. I must stay strong.*

I just needed to get through this night and keep my own free will. After all, I had faced these endless nights, time after time, alone. So, with optimistic thoughts of help coming my way, I continued to endure the relentless battering to my ever-fading spirit.

Chapter 10

Reverend John

I woke as usual after only having a few hours' sleep. The sunset filled my eyes with the glory of daylight, rising with an optimistic feeling of hope and mental freedom of this new day. The banishment of this entity from my life lightens my heart. The thought of going to bed and having silence, clear air and a nontoxic atmosphere is something most of you wouldn't even acknowledge as each night falls; it's normally an everyday procedure. For me, this process has been absent for so long, the hope to regain this natural occurrence will bring the feeling of peace back into my life.

With the knowledge of visitors coming to the house later that afternoon, mum cleaned my room for the hundredth time, ready for Reverend John and his colleague's arrival. I had also seen Steve the previous day and explained everything to him. He insisted that he was there for support, and I welcomed the idea with open arms. Steve arrived just before midday so that he could have lunch with us and be by my side. Poor Dad couldn't hide how nervous and uncomfortable he was. He fidgeted most of the day, moving from room to room, not really knowing what to do with himself.

"Are you ok, love?" He would repeatedly say, a concerned look upon his face.

"Yes, Dad. I'm fine, thanks for asking."

I was not fine, but I didn't want to upset him anymore. All I could do was sit with Steve, watching television for hours. Butterflies

46

were fluttering about in my tummy, desperately waiting for them to arrive.

I was in the living room when I heard the tell-tale signal of the back gate clicking shut, and it was then that I knew they were here. With a determined, strong knock at the door, in they walked. Reverend John introduced his five accompanying colleagues to us all and proceeded to explain the outline of how the evening would go. All five of his church colleagues came dressed in casual wear; the reverend, on the other hand, stood proudly from head to toe in his holy attire.

Reverend John looked around impatiently and cleared his throat. "Are we ready? Let's begin."

This was it: the final instruction for the night's exorcism.

Before anything else happened, I felt a hand on my shoulder. As I looked around, I could see it was Reverend John. No words were exchanged, only the gaze from his eyes to mine. This told me all I needed to know. I was no longer alone in this battle.

With some trepidation, I led them to my bedroom. As we entered, I could hear them muttering between themselves. They all stood in silence, looking around, taking in everything visual and invisible whilst intermittently glancing over to one another. As they did this, Reverend John advised that I opened my bedroom window as wide as it could go. This would allow the demonic entity to leave through the window without causing any more damage than it may have already done. He then suggested that we arrange ourselves into a circle, holding on to the hands of the person next to us.

Standing together, Reverend John began reciting the Lord's Prayer. The meaning and love behind every word filled the room. As the recitation finished, we continued to stand in unity for the next stage of the process. By this point, I could feel the sweat building in the palms of my hands as the anxiety inside of me mounted.

On opening my eyes from the prayer, I noticed Reverend John grasping a wooden crucifix in his hand. He held this out into the space of my room and began speaking the words from the exorcism prayer. As he spoke, the conviction in his voice was apparent, the prominence of his actions made known. As his voice echoed around my room, you could feel the instant changes in the air.

The start of heavy, musty breaths penetrated down my neck as the entity began to show its persistent presence. You could feel the building of an accumulating wind that circled between us. The sounds of a devilish growl entwined within it. As I looked over to Steve, Mum and Dad, I could see their fearful expressions etched on their faces. I knew with no doubt that the entity was here amongst us. You could feel the anger within it as it moved ever closer. As the exorcism prayer continued, each word antagonised and rivalled the presence of the entity.

The intensity within my room grew with every passing minute. The continual whistling from the howling wind wrapped itself around each and every one of us. You could feel the coldness of the air as it whipped against your exposed skin. The same dampened bonfire smell followed the rush of wind as it circulated. As the entity force heightened, so did the sounds of electricity clicking, echoing from every corner of the room.

As Reverend John continued to read the words from the exorcism prayer, the pressure within the room intensified to such a degree it was impossible to ignore. Growling noises with unearthly tones were sweeping past our ears, evoking fear through to the depths of our souls. It felt like the demonic entity was becoming ever stronger. The fight between us was clear. The persistence in its dominance to override the situation was fraught.

For a split second, I felt as though I was looking down from the ceiling at everyone, the circumstance in which we were in this very night, the constant reminders of my fear, everything. It seemed so mind-blowing, even though I have lived for days and years with the fact that this has been my reality. Why was this happening to me? Will I ever be free? The growing fear of how this would end troubled my mind. How was this demonic entity going to react to its demise? I had witnessed first-hand the capabilities and strength it has within itself over the last few years, which left me unsure as to whether the little fight I have left inside is enough to complete the task.

With the continual mantra of words spoken from the warning prayer, there was this heavy pressure within our heads; the feeling was very uncomfortable. Like an intense squeezing, a tightened band that got tighter and tighter. A vice-like grip. It was difficult to ignore, but we knew we had to show a determination of strength together. To stand up against the forceful attempts in breaking us down.

I was ever conscious of the feeling from the entity's stare against my face as it circled me with its dominance. It wasn't going to leave me without a fight. With my weakened mind and body, I was wavering fast. I knew I had to dig deeper than I had ever before; staying strong was the only way out of this. If I gave in now, I would never live a life without the ongoing torment of this demon.

It hated the strength that we had incapsulated amongst the circle of which we stood. It continued endlessly to badger my thought process. I had to stay focused.

Every one of us present could feel the immensity of this demon as it circled amongst us all. Reverend John began anointing holy water around and within the circle we stood. The determination was etched on his face. The holy words spoken cut the atmospheric air like a knife. The eerie groaning sounds seemed to come from every crevice of my room, and the gripping of our hands tightened all the more in defiance. You could feel and hear the boundless mass of erratic energy bouncing from the walls, crackling like bolts of lightning. The intensity in the air was like a volcano ready to erupt; it was indescribable.

With my room filled with unimaginable sights and sounds, Reverend John gave the nod to be ready for the final part of the exorcism. To rid my life of this demon. Standing boldly and omitting a power of strength beyond his clerical collar, he began instructing the demon present to leave the house. As he did this, aggressive knocks to our bodies were being felt, with a painful popping of the ears from the mounting pressure.

Whilst this was all happening, I became aware of a thick, black-ish-grey smoke travelling low to the floor that had begun to entwine itself around our feet. You could feel every ounce of energy within it. Loud banging sounds started emerging from the walls, door and the floor on which we stood. The vibration from the bangs wobbled up through our bodies. The same howling wind thrashed around the room like a torrent, moving our hair like we were in a wind tunnel.

As I watched the efforts of this demon fighting the words from the bible, an immense force came from behind us, pushing us forward, causing our footing to move. Suddenly, my curtains were thrust out the window with such power that the railing was also pulled from the wall and hit the floor with a thud.

Reverend John slowly lowered his crucifix to his side. The room fell to a deadly silence. A deafening stillness that was brand new to me. I glanced over to Reverend John.

"Is it over?" I said, trembling, fearful of his answer.

My mouth was so dry I could barely speak. We all looked around at each other, waiting for him to speak. All the while, Steve was still holding on tightly to my hand.

"It's gone. It's over." Reverend John said calmly.

It was then, in that long-awaited moment, that I knew the demon had left. Strangely, I didn't know what to think or how to feel at that point. I looked over to Reverend John and saw a look of triumph on his face. It had been a night from hell. We all stood motionless for a while. Reverend John's colleagues were all breathing a sigh of relief that the night was finally over. The immediate lightness in the air could be felt by everyone.

Before they gathered their garments to leave, Reverend John cupped my hands within his once again and said with a warm smile, "You will be safe now, child. May your faith stay strong and continue to rise above the darkness that exists within this world."

Those words will forever be carved in my memory, and I will always be eternally thankful to the reverend and his colleagues who accompanied him that night. I had gone through absolute turmoil for a number of years with this entity terrorising my life night after night. Then suddenly, it was gone. The shoes in which I stood seemed alien to me. I felt ecstatic beyond words at the thought of finally being free of the terror, but was I really free of it? This was an ongoing battle I had with myself.

After Reverend John and his colleagues from the church had left, Dad brought to our attention that he had noticed an uncomfortable burning sensation coming from around his calf muscles just before the end of the exorcism. As Dad pulled up his trouser leg to show us, both Mum and I could see what looked like friction burns on the back of one of his legs. They looked red and sore. How Dad became inflicted with these burns, none of us can be certain. The one fact we can be sure of is that Dad did not have these prior to the exorcism.

Later that night, even though I had been given the guarantee from Reverend John that the demonic presence had been expelled, I felt a strangeness looming over my head. No matter how often I continually gave myself some reassurance, the feeling would not budge. This I have found difficult to express. It wasn't at all that I didn't have trust in the comforting words that had been spoken to me, as I had complete faith in everything that Reverend John and his fellow members had done that night. It was more of a case that something just didn't feel right.

In bed, I tried my best to shrug off this negative sense that I felt. I could instantly feel that the air in my room felt so much lighter and clearer than it once had; nevertheless, there was some kind of undercurrent to what I was sensing. Was there still a presence of some description looming around? I immediately began praying to Jesus, asking him to surround my family and our home with his love and protection. I was desperately holding on to the hope of living free from any fear from this night on.

As I tried to lay within the peace of the night, I couldn't help but notice the ongoing sense of not being alone. I knew I was being watched; I could feel it. This inner sense I had become accustomed to and knew well. Understandably my fear began bubbling up once again. I couldn't believe I was feeling this way. It had only been a few hours since Reverend John had left.

As that night passed by, it brought nothing more than my sense of being watched. The presence I felt could well have been a heavenly spirit bringing its normal ethos.

The following nights felt pretty much the same, being made aware that I was not totally alone. The atmospheric changes in the air were nothing like what I had experienced with the demonic manifestation. These were much lighter, calmer and brought forth a different presence altogether.

Everything was so much better and easier now. My crazy, heightened fear had settled down to a more normal level. Instead, I now had unanswered questions in my head that followed me every day. Why did I have to experience this? This experience had turned my life upside down. The aftermath of this, for me, was why? I am a good person with good morals, so why did this demon come into my life and wreak havoc?

I needed to try and find some answers; it was one of the first and last things I thought about. It was starting to send me mad. Had I somehow gone down the wrong pathway, which had led me to this? I understand that I will never get a completely definitive answer as that's impossible, but to be able to be told the possible reasons, if any, would maybe ease my mind.

Let's face it; this was not an everyday occurrence in people's lives. It wouldn't be a topic of conversation that I could bring up over a coffee with anyone, apart from my family. People would either think I'm deluded or had gone completely mad. I had good friends around me that maybe I could have spoken to, but I decided against doing that. I was so afraid of the possible detriment to my character, of who I am. Could you imagine some of the Chinese whispers that would have been said by some people hearing this information?

For the majority of people, these experiences are played out by actors in a film with viewing lasting a matter of hours, then forgotten. For me, no actors were present; this was as real as it gets.

Chapter 11

Lessons from the Wiser

With my ongoing yearning for answers, I turned to a wonderful lady that I had met through Steve. She had been a prominent elder in his life, outside of his family. Anne had lived with her partner Fred in the same block of flats as Steve's parents. They owned an Alsatian called Prince, and Steve, being only twelve at the time, fell in love with him and often took the dog for a walk. His relationship with Anne grew over the years, and they became great friends.

Anne always looked out for Steve, giving him homemade baked treats in return for the dog walks. Anne was a wise individual. She had many hidden talents regarding mediumship that I was unaware of at the time.

On one visit, I took it upon myself to open up and discuss some of the events I had been through whilst enjoying an afternoon's tea with her. By this time, Anne and Fred had moved to a warden assisted property due to Fred's worsening disabilities.

I had always felt very comfortable in Anne's company. Her soft-spoken voice and open arms gave me an instant comforting feel, which enabled me to discuss the subject with someone outside of my immediate family. I was interested in what Anne would make of it all. With my seemingly endless chat, I noticed there were no facial expressions of surprise or doubt from her. She just sat and listened intently to my every word. It didn't matter what I said, she continued with the same attentive, endearing look. By now, we had drunk a few cups of tea and eaten through half of the Victoria sponge that had kindly been laid out on her little wooden table in the kitchen for us to share.

After I had said all I'd wished to say, Anne, in her calming manner, began to tell me that she had also experienced many encounters of the spiritual nature in her time. Hearing this gave me a strange sense of belonging, and I felt an eagerness to listen to more from her. She sat there on her wooden chair, looking at me fondly through the occasional puff of cigarette smoke. Her mousey brown hair sat just above her shoulders, framing her round face that always radiated love and joy. Anne continued to express that there was more to life than what we see in front of us. It is my belief that everybody has the ability to see and hear messages from the spirit world. Their higher senses are enough for them to feel and know what's there. However, there is only a percentage of people who allow themselves to believe this is possible. Others often need physical proof in order to believe anything more than what stands in front of them. It's all to do with opening your subconscious mind to the spiritual realm.

I became totally encapsulated by Anne's words. I had never heard of it put into this context before. My eagerness to hear more was plain to see. From that point on, I had a kindred bond with her. I knew there was something different about Anne, but I couldn't put my finger on it. As an elderly lady, she had an air about her and the manner in which she carried herself. Now it was becoming clear to me that maybe Anne was going to hold some if not all of the answers I sought.

We broke from the subject for a while and took a walk around her garden. She fed an array of wild animals at the same time every day, and nothing was allowed to interfere with the scheduled feeding. Nothing was too much trouble for her when it came down to the animals. She showered them with love and attention. After preparing their meals, Anne would place several large bowls filled with sumptuous amounts of food in the exact same place for the animals to feast on each night. It was lovely to witness the assortment of wild animals freely eating and playing within the grounds of her garden. Some of which ate with no hesitation from her hand. All animals, whether wild or domestic, gave Anne so much pleasure in her life.

After witnessing the nightly feasting, we ended up back in the kitchen to continue with our conversation. Here, Anne went on to tell me that life had not always gone how she had planned. Unfortunately, having to face up to a life without children came as a huge blow to her. But, instead of dwelling on her misfortune, she and her husband ran a children's home for many years - until they were unable to do so anymore. The children's home gave Anne not one or two children but many, which she relished in. I can't help but think how lucky those children were to have had such a caring lady looking after them. She really was one of the most generous people I have ever met in my life. She always thought of others.

I often wondered if Anne ever felt lonely, as she had no other siblings and had lost both of her parents at a young age. She had her husband, of course, but with no other family members to call on, it made me wonder. So, I put that question to her.

With a swift response, she said, "I have an array of company every day, from those that dwell beyond the glass wall that divides us on the earth plane to those that are living around me. I am very rarely ever alone."

I couldn't help but smile hearing this.

With that, Anne continued to express the gratitude from the spirit world for the company they bring her each and every day.

"None of us are ever really alone in this world," she told me. "Neither are we alone on the other side."

Captivated, I asked her to tell me more. I learnt that in her younger years, she had become aware of the people around her that others could not see. With the bombardment from many spirits, Anne went on to help others by connecting passed loved ones with the living, giving members of the public comfort whenever needed. I could see in the way she spoke that this had given her great enjoyment over the years, and she felt a sense of fulfilment in being able to do so.

As I listened on, I could feel the selfless way in which she was divulging her past to me, trying to help answer some of the questions I had put to her. With this knowledge, I knew it would be fine to open up to Anne about my fearful nights with the visitations from the demonic manifestation. I knew I could tell her how, since the exorcism had been performed, I had a constant sense of being watched. I had also been having some new physical symptoms of an ongoing heavy head and frequent dizzy spells that were intrusive on certain days, often becoming debilitating.

"Come and see me tomorrow," she said beaming, softly rubbing my arm for comfort. "I'll take you to see my friend that I have known for many years. Her name is Mel. She will be able to help you to settle, and this is what I think you require at this time. You can trust her implicitly with any questions you have regarding your past experiences."

I pondered long and hard that evening at home, wary of opening myself up to yet another person outside of my family. But I trusted Anne and knew deep down that she would not be introducing me to anyone that she did not have faith and trust in. After all, this is what I wanted.

Early afternoon the following day, Steve and I met Anne at her house. Not knowing where we were going, Anne drove us to Mel's. On arrival, we parked alongside an old lime stoned wall; behind it stood a few small cottages. We followed on behind Anne. As we opened the little wooden gate to the entrance of the home, I could see a silhouette of a lady standing at the window. When we knocked at the door, the same lady greeted us with an invitation to enter her home. As we entered, I could sense a tweak in the air. Mel introduced herself and led us to a lounge/dining room area. We sat around a small wooden table covered with a lace tablecloth. To the side of the table sat a lit lamp; it gave off a warm glow to the room through the red tasselled lampshade. After making a pot of tea, Mel joined us. She was of an older generation, small in height, with a rounded figure. She wore her long grey hair in a ponytail, with a bright red scrunchy tied round it.

Mel sat at the opposite side of the table, facing me. With a smile on her face, she proceeded in asking me a number of questions in reference to my visit. Cautiously, I disclosed some details of my present and previous experiences. I found the same nagging question in my head, interrupting again and again as I spoke to Mel. This pivotal question was WHY me? WHY did I have to go through this? WHY did I have to experience the ongoing torment from a demonic entity? So, with this opportunity, I put this question to her.

With the breath of a long sigh, Mel responded.

"With asking why, you're holding on to past events. Why is a wondering word that can't always be answered. Go forward now. Don't keep asking yourself why. These events happened, and when you have no answer to your pondering, it stains your forward-thinking, keeping you locked in the past. Let it all go, move on. It's unhealthy to hold on to such negative baggage. The one thing you should be focusing on is what hidden courage, strength, and ability you had within yourself to stand up to such an experience. Turn it around, and use this as a positive. Help others to find the courage to speak up and not to be afraid. This experience has given you a key of wisdom in this field. Use this by helping others to not suffer in silence. The consistent knowledge you have built over the years can help break down any despair and loneliness that one may be feeling. Show them that they can overcome this plight in the same way you once did. Sometimes you have to fight to find the light."

At first, I felt a little disappointed with her answer. It wasn't until I gave more thought to the words that Mel had spoken to me, did I realise the purpose and meaning of what was said. Even though this process has been a long and enduring task, I have, and I am finally taking my dark and deepest experiences forward as a positive. The most positive aspect is writing this book. It's with all my love and hope that if any part of this book resonates with any of you, that you, too, can find your strength within and stand strong. Rise out from the other end even stronger than you were before. At the time, I know this might seem like an unreachable journey. Don't give in to anything you know not to be right.

Mel continued to help me with my dizzy spells and heavy head, with a procedure known as grounding. I had never heard of this before, until that day. I felt comfortable enough in Mel's company to allow the procedure to go ahead. I don't know the ins and outs of what she did, but I do know that at one point, I was unable to lift either of my arms or legs. They felt like ton weights. It was like the floor had swallowed my feet up to my ankles, as though I had walked into some wet cement. Nevertheless, it certainly helped settle my issue of dizzy spells and heavy head. Mel also advised that I help myself to stay grounded. This can simply be done by standing barefoot in the garden and visualising your feet connecting firmly in the ground to mother earth. It sounds crazy, but having done this from time to time, I found it works.

As our conversation flowed from one area to another, I did find some understanding as to the possible reasoning behind the demonic visitations. The possible conclusion is that Satan has the ability to attach himself or other demonic beings from the underworld to any strong, loving connection you have with a loved one that has passed over. This I had, and still have, with my grandma. This could well have been an area that enabled the entity's entry. I have learnt that these demonic entities prey mostly on girls of a certain age, normally of teenage years. Add this to my already opened ability to connect with heavenly spirits, such as my grandad, then my grandma. When mixed with my unintentionally holding on to the passing of my grandma, it enabled it to use these connections in gaining an opening to begin its luring traits.

I know that this all sounds totally absurd and farfetched, but it has a good standing of truth with regards to my own situation. The demon used my profound love to groom me into becoming a follower with the intention of convincing me to do his evil work here on the earth plane. Thank goodness my faith was strong enough to withstand this monstrosity's intrusions.

My first visit became that of many to Mel's house. Each visit was always intuitive, and I learnt a lot from her wisdom within the spiritual field. Both Anne and Mel helped me through my journey over the years, providing me with their endless guidance. Even so, there will always be questions that resonate in my mind as they remain unanswered.

Unfortunately, after a few years had passed and with a saddened heart, both Anne and Mel departed this world within a year of each other. They left me with many of their teachings which maybe one day I will pass on to someone else who's experiencing the same journey who also wish to learn these lessons from the wiser. I was fortunate enough to be able to thank Anne for all of her time and patience in helping me to adjust and to accept my privileges from the spirit world.

I often come across different situations where I wish I still had Anne and Mel to converse with.

Then I remember as Anne once said to me, "Don't try looking too hard for your answers. It will more than likely be standing right in front of you. Open your eyes, and you will see what it is your meant to see."

I often feel their encouragement, the prods to my subconscious mind to always believe in myself and others, even if that comes with much opposition at times.

Chapter 12

Finding My Way

As I went through normal day-to-day life, I would subconsciously be reminded by those that no longer walked the earth plane, those that had ascended into the spirit world. Reminders are everywhere for all of us. Some of us see these reminders with no concerns, others with a fragmented view. This distorted view is created by individuals who block the natural ability with which they are born; this goes for us all. We are all spiritual beings. Not wanting to see or believe the signs which are shown to us from spirits is usually down to your upbringing or influence from non-believers, which taints your thoughts and views.

If your mind allows such thoughts for a moment, they are soon challenged to be just a coincidence or a rationale is provided. However, I believe these signs are deliberately placed in front of us from spirits. These can simply be a recognisable song, to the aroma of perfume or aftershave that brings a recollection of someone to you. When we take the time to acknowledge these moments, we automatically place the individual within our thoughts. This enables your connection to stay between you. With a simple thought, vibrations are omitted that your loved ones in spirit hear and feel.

At this stage of my life, it wasn't a surprise to me to be standing in a queue at a cash register within a busy supermarket, hearing distant muttering of different voices. These voices I now know were not of those doing their weekly shopping but from the spirit realm. At first, this was a little disturbing, but something I soon became accustomed to.

On the first few occasions of noticing this, I would find myself looking over my shoulder, firstly to the right, then to the left, trying to fathom out who I could hear talking. Never wanting to seem rude, I'd ask whoever was with me at the time if I had missed what they had said. If that wasn't the case, I would initially pass it off as picking up on other customers conversations standing close by. However, as these mutterings continued, I realised these voices were not the other shoppers. I found myself tilting my head from side to side in a bid to focus my hearing and in the hope of making their voices clearer. Similar I suppose to when you adjust your television antenna to pick up on better reception. These voices didn't always come one at a time, but sometimes many, all saying something at once. My head would feel like it was buzzing, being filled with a muddled mass of conversation. I often became a little disorientated and had to focus my mind on the job at hand.

On other occasions, these voices came as only one and much clearer. Instinctively, I became drawn to an individual with whom they wished to connect. The idea of approaching these individuals sent my confidence spiralling, and with much discontent, I never approached them. I was so unsure as to how they would accept what I had to say. I did and still do feel as though I let those spirits down. I trust they understood my inexperience and that the situation could have become complicated. I apologised time after time for not passing their message on. However, if I ever received any message from spirit for someone I was more acquainted with, I would always pass it on to them.

Sometimes, a spirit would come through to me in poem mode. I would suddenly hear these flowing words and knew I needed to write them down. If the spirits taught me anything, it was to hold on to their words of guidance, for they could be for the here and now or for a day we have not yet reached. Their poems were always beautiful, the words meaningful but light. Dependent on the day, I wouldn't always read them immediately, as I found their message much clearer to see at a later date. Still to this day, I have kept all of the poems gifted to me. They're a reminder of my contact with those spirits of that time.

One of my aunts on my mums' side was a regular visiting figure in my parents' home. She became very interested in the different stories I would tell her and some of the spiritual contacts I have had. She loved reading the poems and became transfixed if I felt spirit with us at that particular moment. I found most of the spirit contact made to me was just that, contact. They seemed to enjoy being able to make some vibrational contact with us here on the earth plane. Not necessarily for any reason, but to forward information that most of the time had no significance to the time or place I was at.

With time being of no relevance to those in the spirit realm, they often presented themselves or items from their era. In these such cases, I would turn to my parents for some help in clarifying what it was certain spirits were showing me. After some lengthy, detailed descriptions, my understanding of the presented image would become clearer. These images would pop up out of nowhere, transmitted through my mind's eye. The easiest way to explain this is it's like having a photograph flashed in front of your eyes, but instead of seeing it with your eyes, the image is firmly placed in your head.

For instance, I used to see this extremely smart gentleman, dressed perfectly in a brown uniform, proudly showing the medals on one side of his chest. He had a super moustache that curled up at the end and wore the smallest round glasses. He never made any attempt to converse in any way. He stood tall with a refined posture. A hardened facial expression that somehow didn't fit what I think was his true personality. I always acknowledged his presence and how smartly dressed he was. He stood with a sense of proudness, and so he should, being one of the many gentlemen that fought for our country. It was always an amazing and privileged experience when they presented themselves to me like that.

Apart from a handful of times, I continued to keep these experiences within my family. I had been told many times to sit within a spiritual circle to enhance my ability, but I never did. Fear of people's views was always my problem, and I wasn't really sure that I wanted to expand my ability any further or to any degree. Keeping everything to how it was, was the simplest way. I didn't feel the need to enhance my ability from what I had already seen, heard and felt. More to the point, I had already kept so much of who I was a secret from nearly all of my friends and colleagues. Adding something else was just too tiresome for me. All that I carried was more than enough. I hated the prospect of people finding out what I had experienced, then looking at me differently from who they thought I once was. Deep down, I knew that this would be the exact reaction from some of the people I called friends. They wouldn't be able to see through the fact that I was still the same person, just a holder of unexplained privileges.

Over the years, I heard the mutterings of disapproval from Joe Public on such issues many times. Often their views come from fear. Fear and doubt close your eyes to the wider picture. I find the walls of disbelief that some people build difficult to understand because of everything that I have experienced over the years. However, I suppose, on the other hand, they could say the same.

Chapter 13

Through the Years

As the chapter states, time has passed by.

I married Steve, and we have since had two daughters. Both of them have made us very proud parents over the years. They shine brightly in their own individual ways. We've always been a very close family and spend quality time together a few days every week. As the girls grew into fine young women, they also had families of their own, enhancing our family network with beautiful grandchildren. Thankfully, the closeness we have with our girls has led to a fantastic bond with each and every one of them. The light they have in their eyes brightens any grey day. Their open minds fascinate me, accepting everything that comes their way. We should all take some teachings from toddler minds and learn to accept all walks of life, no matter how different they may be.

We all judge too quickly these days. There seems to be no middle ground in the way we try to learn and accept the differences of others around us. If only we did, it would be a good work in progress. Why don't we look at the differences as integral parts played in this world? Judgement is a component of fear. Not understanding someone or something makes most of us start building comparisons. We can learn so much from each other if only we try to accept all walks of life. We're not supposed to think the same way. Every one of us has a part to play, a piece of the puzzle to place in the universe.

* * *

As both the girls grew, they also experienced different aspects of the spirit world. Up to this point, I had not mentioned anything to them about what I had been through over the years. So, this was purely their own spiritual experiences. A couple of these experiences were visual, which was distressing at times for them both. On one of these visitations, they saw what they described as a blue lady hovering over my bed in mid-air. Neither of them could see her face but could relate in some detail that she was wearing a blue coloured dress that flowed like it was blowing in the wind as she hovered face down above my bed. This particular spirit never made herself known to me, only the girls. Her reason for showing herself to them both is unclear.

On another occasion, a dark shadow of a man made himself known to them every night over a number of days. They both remember these visitations clearly to this day. He would stand on our landing, just outside the entrance to the girl's bedroom. Sometimes they would see him walk up and down the landing, occasionally stopping by their door as if he was looking in on them. Whenever the girls had these visions from spirit, I would be called upon throughout the night to settle their understandable apprehension.

It was a difficult subject to explain, but I did so the only way I knew how: to be honest. They were both at an age where I could engage in conversation with them. So, their lessons began early, to understand that spirits are around us all the time, without even knowing it. I tried my best to explain that just because life has ended on the earth plane, it doesn't mean the spirit living within the body has died too. Spirits' love for communication is still the same as when they were here in body. This is especially so with their loved ones - the bonds we make never fade.

As the girls got older in years, I did tell them about my long history with spiritual contact. However, I left out the true extent of the mental torment that I endured from the darker side of the outer realm. Instead, this I will leave in the contents of this book. It will be their own decision as to whether they wish to read it or not, as it is with you all.

If I've taught my girls anything, it is to live life to the full and always with joy and love in their hearts. Not to judge or be judged, because, at the end of the day, we are all trying to do the best we can. Believe in yourself always, be happy and content with the person that looks back at you from the glass in the mirror. Finally, carry yourself with an open mind to all the possibilities that exist in this world.

Chapter 14

Having Faith in Your Hands

As I come to the final chapter of my book, I'm hopeful I have encouraged a thought process that has fired up your own realisation journey to believe more exists out there than what your eyes see. Be this from the similarities in our experiences or purely the interest in what others have experienced paranormally. In turn, this broadens your once restricted mind to all possibilities in this and the other world.

I'm a firm believer that we all are capable of interaction with spirits; it's all dependant on whether you wish to. Most of us seek higher guidance for reassurance that we're doing or wanting to do the right thing most days. Either by prayer or in silent thought, the spirit hears it all. This may be in times of need, for example, when all other avenues have been covered. We may lift up and ask for help, which for some may not always be answered. This is when we have the tendency to doubt that anything's out there listening.

However, remember when faltering, this is your journey, not theirs - you alone hold the key to your destinations in life. We should think more about listening to our own self-guidance within our subconscious. We're wired with this from the time conception takes place, but it is often ignored. It often presents itself with a niggling feeling in the pit of your stomach. Your gut instinct. If we were to take note of what our bodies are telling us in certain dilemmas, we would answer our own questions the majority of the time. If, for some reason, we make an incorrect choice in that moment, then why not look at it as a lesson learned rather than a failing? None of us can fail in life unless we choose to. That decision is yours and yours alone to make. Life is set out in such a way that we can attempt to do whatever it is we desire, numerous times, if necessary, until we succeed. The world is your oyster.

I'm thankful for all my experiences, even the toughest of situations that I have had to face. They have made me realise that no matter the enormity of my struggles and fears, there will always be light at the end of the tunnel. We all have a silent warrior that lies within, that enables us to muster that determination to overcome all that stands in our way. Have faith always; you're stronger than you think you are.

Over time, these enormities that I have come across with facing the chapters of paranormal existence, good and bad, have finally given me a voice that I am no longer afraid to express. This voice is now content and strong enough to open up and divulge all that I know to be factual. I am no longer afraid of the thoughts and views of any members of the disbelieving opposition.

Lately, my knowledge and experience have come in handy for one of my granddaughters. Being of a very young age, it was of paramount importance that I try to help her in the best way I know how. She was waking during the night, screaming with terror at the unwelcomed strangers she was seeing. These manifestations would appear in her room day or night. In her bedroom, the kitchen, everywhere around the house. I could instantly see how frightened she was, and understandably so. The situation had become intolerable for her and her parents, who had much concern seeing the actions their young daughter took to try and get away from the visions she was seeing.

One evening in particular, whilst sitting in their dining room eating their evening meal, my daughter noticed CeCe was hanging her head down low; her hair had fallen forward, covering the sides of her face. Her parents made every effort in getting to lift her head; even her little brother's chatter did nothing to change the matter. The next thing was CeCe had slowly slid down her chair and assembled herself in a ball-like state, hiding under the dining table. This was very alarming for my daughter; she was nothing like her usual bubbly self.

When my daughter was finally able to coax her out from the table, CeCe began screaming a horrible, pitiful scream. Holding her arm out straight, pointing directly in front of her, she started crying out, complaining of a lady that was standing in the doorway, staring at her. Instinctively, my daughter realised what was going on and called to see if I could travel up to their house with some urgency.

As I arrived, I could see little CeCe was troubled by the expression on her face. I picked her up and gave her a reassuring hug. I tried settling her whilst I listened to her mum's account of what had been happening of late. Everything that was being said in conversation between us was done in such a way that CeCe wouldn't realise the topic of discussion.

As my daughter continued explaining the unusual events, it became apparent that a few strange things had been going on in the house too. However, it wasn't until now that she was able to piece them all together so that it made sense. She explained situations like a prominent coldness surrounding her whilst washing up; the circulating air was chilly enough to cause goose pimples to pop up and down her arms. As I sat listening intently, she expressed that she had also become aware of a shadow passing behind her the other day while she was ironing, but whenever she had turned to see what it was that caught her eye, nothing was there.

With this information in mind, I decided to ask what CeCe could tell me about the lady. Even though she was young, she was able to converse very well. Having a close relationship with all of my grandchildren, I felt that maybe she would trust that her grandma was here to help. As I began to question CeCe, she continued looking agitated and fearful. At first, she didn't seem at all happy to say much about the lady to me, but after a while, CeCe began explaining that this lady suddenly appears and stands looking at her. She will either appear looking around the door frame of their pantry or suddenly manifesting by the dining room chairs as they sit down to eat. As she continued to express herself, she began gingerly looking around the room with a wary expression. She was afraid that continuing to mention this lady would make her appear again.

As CeCe looked into my eyes, I could see that she wanted to tell me something. I probed further with encouragement to speak up, and I felt my stomach churning with upset seeing her looking so afraid.

With a whispering voice, she said to me, "Make her go away, Grandma; I don't like her."

I knew I needed to sort this situation out for CeCe. The sooner, the better. I was hoping that the lady spirit would present herself while I was there, allowing me to connect with her and request that she move on to another place. At this point, there was nothing much more I could do. I did, however, bring her my brown teddy bear as a comforter, which my husband had brought me as a valentine's gift some years ago. I had become aware of her interest in this particular bear after spotting it sitting on top of my wardrobe. It was so soft and squishy; the hope was it would give CeCe something else to focus on.

Before I left that evening, I passed CeCe the bear, kissed her on the forehead and said, "Cuddle my bear whenever you're afraid. He will keep you safe and sound."

At the time, it seemed to do the trick, which was a relief. Before I left, I made sure I recited the Lord's Prayer, giving an extra protective barrier around them all.

As I drove home, I could sense that this would not be the last time I would be called upon. I certainly felt a presence in the house when I entered but thought it advisable not to elaborate on this too much, as I didn't want to cause anymore apprehension than what was already there.

A few days had passed, and thankfully I had not heard of any disturbances. So, I decided to go up to their house to see if I could feel any presence still lingering as I had done previously, and more importantly, to catch up on how CeCe had been. After a bite to eat and refreshments,

I went upstairs to CeCe's bedroom to play with her for a short while. As we played with her toy kitchen, I saw CeCe beginning to act in a strange manner. Seeing this, I became reminded of what her mother had said to me previously. As I watched, she continued hanging her head low, tilting it round at an angle. It didn't take much working out to see that she was trying to obscure her view from whatever it was that she had seen. Moments later, I could see the anxiety building up inside her. She became so anxious that tears soon followed, cascading down her flushed cheeks, and she was asking frantically to go downstairs. I picked her up and held her close to me; she felt hot and sweaty with panic.

"What is it that you're seeing?" I asked calmly.

I found it very strange that I could not see anything, only feel the obvious change in the atmosphere. As she looked at me with worry, her little face flushed, I knew I needed to keep her with me for as long as I could. Even though I was acutely aware of the need for escape pounding through CeCe's body, the importance of keeping her with me was paramount, no matter how much I wanted to give her the escape route she desired. I knew by now that running from a spirit solves nothing.

A normally chatty child had become silent, which stirred an array of feelings deep inside for me. I had to compose my own emotions the best I could. The feeling of anger was simmering away, being ignited all the more in seeing the fear surfacing in CeCe. However, in circumstances such as these, emotions running riot would help nothing. So, keeping a level head, I managed to distract her focus for a while by paying particular attention to a new addition to her already abundant collection of LOL dolls.

Although the distraction was working well, I noticed CeCe repeatedly looking towards the area of her doorway. I desperately wanted to ask her why but decided against highlighting any previous concerns, especially as it had taken some enticing in getting CeCe to stay and interact. As we continued playing, I positioned myself so that my back was facing the entrance to her bedroom, and suddenly, a blanket of cold air penetrated my jumper. Immediately after feeling this, CeCe reacted with that same stance, tilting her head down low but also, this time, holding her hand up to the side of her face.

"Speak to Grandma," I said. "Tell me what you're seeing."

Eventually, after some persuasion, CeCe explained that the same lady had appeared once again in the doorway to her room, looking in at her. By the time she had finished explaining the whereabouts of the spirit, CeCe had embedded herself in a foetal position in my arms. I could feel her shaking, hot and sweaty as before. This was terrifying her, and the need for action was now. I stood close to where I could feel the presence looming, and with a forceful but polite tone, I spoke out to this particular lady in spirit.

Whenever I speak to a spirit, I'm always courteous and respectful at all times. I tend to give guideline instructions, for example, what perimeter's they can't cross. In this situation, I gave specific instructions to this spirit that she was not to pass the boundary of this bedroom. I also specified that her visual manifestation to this young child has caused a distressing amount of fear, which I'm sure was not her intention. In most cases, they will listen and often move on. So, I was more than hopeful this would be the outcome for CeCe. Having been in this situation on many occasions, I couldn't stress enough to my daughter the importance of making sure she listens to CeCe intently, always showing acknowledgement to what she has to say on the subject. It's a lonely and fearful place to stand alone.

I was called a few more times here and there since that day, with similar manifestations and objects being moved, but thankfully for CeCe's sake, of late, things seem to have settled for the time being. She is still very young, with possibilities as she becomes older of igniting the opening for more channelling from the spirit world. Only time will tell. The one certainty is that if she is to follow the path of contact from the higher world, I will be standing right by her side, giving a helping hand along her journey.

In most cases, spirits are just looking in on us from an observational aspect, but because our teachings from the time of birth are confined to such a degree, we believe that death brings a complete end. For people such as myself who have had so many experiences with spirit, we know this cannot be so. We are all made from an energy force that feeds and emits vibrations to and from the universe. This is eternal.

When we choose to be born, whether this is for the first or second time, it is our own choice to walk the earth plane in our designated shells for human existence. Or, our passage through life's journey enables us to achieve the highest form of spiritual enlightenment, which means you may prefer to be of guidance from the heavenly realm for the living. It is only our human bodies that decay and wither after enduring our earthly existence. Our spirit self leaves and returns to our natural higher place. It's all about enhancing our spirituality, whether this is religion-based or by the willingness to expand your perspective beyond what stands in front of you.

Faith, health, trust and happiness are the four components we need to function well within this world. These sources we ignite from the moment we open our eyes from our night's slumber. You are Intermittently firing millions of impulses that surge through your body, sending out those frequency waves of vibrations into the universe. Too often, you allow non-conforming views from those around you to lower your vibrational frequency, creating congestion within your inner flow. You need to trust your own thought process in the decisions you make, go with your instincts in what you believe to be right, and hold that faith you have in yourself firmly in your hands.

Just before I closed my laptop in the completion of this book, I felt compelled to write one last paragraph.

Along with my own inner strength, I'm not sure how I would have got through a lot of my experiences without the guidance and protection from the heavens. My faith has always been there, even as a young child, but after my encounters with the horrifying satanic manifestation, it became one of my main support systems, which I held on to with dear life. The love, protection and guidance got me through those unimaginable times of my life. I will be forever grateful because, without this higher intervention, I'm sure I would not be the same person I am today. In saying that, this is in no way a form of manipulation to be a believer, nor in fact, to believe anything that I have written in this book. We have our own free will, each and every one of us. We will make our own decisions. It wouldn't be right for us all to have the same beliefs, so no matter what conclusion you come to, neither one of us is right or wrong.

Printed in Great Britain
by Amazon

77167775R00050